Pastor Jeff Clark bringing awareness, through trial and error, to the truth behind, "This is the way, walk in it." Jeff will take you on an honest journey from, as he puts it, "emerging from the tunnels of [his] soul's imprisonment" to "the reality of a loving and just Father." Jeff moves us from "lostness" to "sustained joy" in life in just 148 pages. For the Jesus-loving sojourner looking for a place that provides fresh and life-giving Manna —Good News—*Communion Disciple* is that place. Enjoy!

—**Fred Antonelli, Ph.D., LPC**
President, Elim Bible Institute and College

Get ready to read a great story! But you're going to get more than just the intriguing twists and turns of Jeff Clark's story; you're also going to see—from the example of Jeff's life—what it really means to follow Jesus as His disciple. You're about to identify the next steps you need to take to give Jesus your *everything*.

—**Bob Sorge**
Author, *Secrets of the Secret Place*

I love reading discipleship books, especially when they describe the process the Lord takes someone through to mold and shape them for ministry. It is something you never forget—something that shapes whatever you do in the future. That is what this book will do for you. Jeff Clark tells the story of what happened to him as a young disciple whose life and ministry have been indelibly marked by those early days of following Jesus. His later work in missions and pastoral ministry, his being able to hear the voice of God for others, his becoming the president of a Bible college, and even his being a father and a strong family man—all comes out of his early discipleship experience. Jeff has been marked by the humbling and honesty, the pain and perplexity, and the submission and surrender he writes about in this book. He has excelled at various kinds of ministry, but I think what he is most effective at doing is helping others navigate their own dealings in discipleship.

—**Penn Clark**
Pastor, WellSpring Fellowship
Author, *Jesus Is Still Making Disciples Today*

Communion Disciple

One Man's Sojourn in Following Jesus

Jeff Clark

Cover design by Laurel Heiser
Edited by Edie Mourey

ISBN: 979-8-9880114-0-8 (print)

ISBN: 979-8-9880114-1-5 (e-book)

❀ Created with Vellum

This book is dedicated to the One who stands at the door of our hearts and knocks. He promises, "If anyone hears My voice and opens the door, I will come into him and dine with him, and he with Me" (Revelation 3:20).

Contents

Foreword

The Communion Disciple is a critical addition for your library. This is how every book on discipleship should be written: as a reflection of one's own path and the life lessons of Abba Father along the way!

Jeff Clark has put his finger on one of the premier issues in the Church today—discipleship—or rather the lack thereof. There is an upward call to biblical discipleship, one that can progress in the life of every believer if they are willing. I hear the Spirit's urgent call to see biblical discipleship in the Church, the way it was supposed to be. But the Church of today is swelled to its brim with what Jeff refers to as "carnal disciples"—those who have come to believing faith but spend most of their days in a state of immaturity, never learning to be a companion of the Lord let alone a communing disciple who hears His voice!

With vivid, humorous, and memorable experiences, Jeff's assessment of his own journey as a disciple of the Lord will resonate resoundingly with all who read this book because we've all been there or are there still. But there is a greater call! It's one for which our Savior bled and died! Jeff has brought the modern crisis of discipleship wildly into focus. The test for all of us now is what will we do about it?

This book is for any believer in any stage of the journey. It will give godly, faithful, and fatherly counsel to those who are still finding their way. The astute among them will avoid many pitfalls and trips around the mountain if they follow its instruction. And its words will be an affirming and encouraging support and blessing to those who are further down the Way.

It's been my great joy to drink in the wisdom of this book, and I commend it to you with all sincerity. I see my own need to continue to press toward the mark. May the Holy Spirit use the words on these pages to sow seeds in you that will reap bountiful fruit for the Kingdom as you pursue the honorable call of the communion disciple.

—Jeffrey D. Crawford
Senior Pastor, All Peoples Church

That which was from the beginning, which we have heard, which we have seen with our eyes, which we have looked upon, and our hands have handled, concerning the Word of life—the life was manifested, and we have seen, and bear witness, and declare to you that eternal life which was with the Father and was manifested to us—that which we have seen and heard we declare to you, that you also may have fellowship with us; and truly our fellowship is with the Father and with His Son Jesus Christ. And these things we write to you that your joy may be full.

— 1 John 1:1–4

Chapter 1

"Come and See"

"SIR, I THINK I'M LOST!" WHEN THOSE WORDS came out of my mouth, I began to cry. The emotion for this four-year-old explorer had reached its peak, and I knew I needed help.

I'll never forget seeing a mailman walking in my direction up the sidewalk and carrying over his shoulder a big leather bag filled with mail. I can still see the letters clutched in his hands as he turned to walk up the sidewalk to the next house, where a woman was on her porch waiting for him. After he handed the mail to the woman standing on her porch, he turned around to return to his Jeep parked at the curb, and I knew then I had to state the facts!

The simple facts were I didn't know where I was and I didn't know where my home was. That's what kicked in the courage to let the mailman know I was lost.

I had only been riding for a short while when I realized I had lost sight of the big, green and yellow moving truck parked in front of our new home. I still remember the huge

Mayflower truck that had pulled up in front of our house in Augusta, Georgia, to load up our family's furniture and haul it down to our awaiting home in New Orleans. My father had accepted a job promotion which meant that our family would be moving from Augusta to New Orleans to begin a new chapter of life together. My memories had begun in that first home, and now new memories would begin in this yet to be discovered house we would be moving into.

As I recall, the truck was so full that the movers had tied our bicycles to the back of the huge trailer. Thankfully, the bikes were still holding on when the truck arrived at the house in New Orleans. I stood back and watched the movers untie the bikes and remove them from the drop-down ramp before they could open the giant doors on the back of the trailer. As they were removing one bicycle after another, one of the workers said to me, "I suppose you are waiting for one of these," to which I happily responded, "Yes, sir, I am."

When my bike was untied and placed in front of me, I immediately jumped on it and began to ride it up and down the sidewalk. I had only recently retired the training wheels and was no doubt focusing on balance more than on my new surroundings. I was oblivious to the fact that I was riding on sidewalks that I was unfamiliar with in a neighborhood that was brand new to me. The house was situated in a cul-de-sac that had a couple of sidewalks connecting it to other cul-de-sacs, each with its own street access in and out.

When I had become aware that I could no longer see the green and yellow truck, I started to retrace my way back home. The more I peddled, the more I began to panic as I realized I did not know where my home was. In merely a few seconds, the panic and fear set in, emotions I don't recall having ever experienced until that moment. My efforts to find my way home were futile, getting me nowhere. That's when I saw the mailman and had to tell him I was lost.

The mailman walked toward me with the concerned look of a father, and the homeowner herself stepped off her porch to come toward me as well. The mailman asked me, "Are you with the family that is moving in where the big Mayflower truck is parked?"

"Yes, sir, I am," I said with tears streaming down my face.

"I know where that is. I can take you there!"

Relief immediately sprang into my panic-and-despair-ridden heart. To really calm my terror, the woman of the house in front of which my meltdown was occurring offered to get me something cold to drink while I sat on the front steps of her porch with the mailman. She soon returned with a sixteen-ounce bottle of Coke and presented the bottle to me. That in itself was amazing, as it was the first time in my young life I had been entrusted with a *full* bottle of Coke! The emotions of the moment were turning a tide as I was being rescued from the peril of having lost my way.

For many years now, I have reflected on that day, the day when as a child I knew I had to acknowledge I was lost in order to get help to find my way. Not to contradict myself, but I had *found myself in lostness*. Lostness. Awkward word, I'll admit, but simply put, it is "the state of being lost." I'm convinced it's a God-given alarm He designed inside us that triggers at different times throughout our lives. It's intended to jump-start the process of being found. It can be a slight nudge like realizing I don't understand the equation my math teacher is explaining, or it can be as dreadful as losing one's way in an unfamiliar neighborhood. Yet its condition can be much larger still in that lostness manifests itself when we begin to question life's meaning, our purpose in life, and our own value.

My childhood story of being lost and then "found" reminds me of what happens when we first encounter our Heavenly Father, the very Creator of the Universe. When we acknowledge we have no clue where we are or why we are here, Holy Spirit steps in like the mailman, as do our brothers and sisters in Christ like the woman on the porch, offering us help and comfort. Once we acknowledge our dreadful state, "I'm lost," Holy Spirit can say, "Come on, I'll show you the way!"

I think sometimes about how different things could have developed that day I ventured off away from the security of my family to chart my own course, if only for a free-wheeling ride on my bicycle. What might have happened had I refused to acknowledge my *lostness* and continued to gamble on my mere will and determination to find my way home? Thankfully, that's not how things went for me, at least not on that day. That day I was sitting on the curb, waiting for the mailman to return to his Jeep, was not the last time I would have to muster the courage to acknowledge my lostness.

With time, we seem to learn how to numb the signals of lostness, ignoring its prompts that we have drifted off course. Like any feeling of insecurity, we can choose to counter its discomfort by pretending to know our way when, in fact, we're drifting further and further from our intended destiny.

The following pages are the result of many years of reflection on the countless miles my miraculous journey with Jesus has taken and the lessons He has taught along the way, *once I admitted I was lost*. My sincere hope is that you would find identity and encouragement cheering you on in your own journey, whether you have or have yet to encounter God for yourself.

From the moment we are made His children by an act of God our Father and His deposit of faith in us to believe, His love compels us to follow His Son as His disciples. Finding our way home would never be realized without Holy Spirit's unique and individual drawing and working in our lives. He does this through His arrangement of circumstances and people along the way that only He can design and orchestrate for each one of us. This is His design and destiny for us in this life, and the most awesome adventure and fulfillment while discovering and experiencing the depth of His love and purpose He has prepared for those who love Him.

Every true follower of Jesus is invited on an exclusive and matchless journey with Him. Together with Him, we proceed through phases of growth, discipline, and ultimate communion. Join me on this journey of incredible personal discovery and purposefulness that is ours as we cling to His invitation and call to *"come and see!"*

Chapter 2

Does Anybody Know Why We're Here?

A LITTLE AFTER MIDNIGHT, TONY AND I HAD JUST dropped off his girlfriend at her apartment, and we were headed home. As we passed in front of City Hall in downtown New Orleans, a blue and white patrol car turned on its lights and siren and pulled us over. As I maneuvered my truck to the curb, the police drew up behind me. I could see in my rearview mirror both doors open and two officers step out of the car.

One officer approached my side of the vehicle while his partner came up along the passenger's side. Each had a flashlight in his left hand with his right hand resting on his service revolver. As I waited for the officer's command, I heard him say, "Both of you step out of the vehicle and stand with your hands behind your heads against the side of the truck."

My truck was a 1966 Chevy panel-truck. I had bought it only the week before, and it was my very first vehicle. It was Tuesday night, and we had had our fill of free drinks, courtesy of another friend who was bartending in a little pub on Rampart Street. Why we chose to drive in front of City Hall that night on our way home is still a mystery to me, but it was the choice we made, and we had to live with it.

In those days, underage consumption of alcohol was winked at where we lived in a city driven by tourism and partying, and law enforcement was more anxious to make arrests for drug possession. We apparently fit the bill, though the term *profiling* was yet to come along a decade or two later. Both of us were long-hairs, or otherwise identified by the police as hippies or street-freaks.

Tony and I got out of the truck and assumed the position. As we stood against the side of the truck, with our hands interlocked behind our heads, one officer frisked our clothing while the other officer began to look through the vehicle. In what seemed to be only seconds, the officer who was looking inside the vehicle returned with a baggie, holding it up before our eyes, and said, "What is this?"

I told him, "I have no idea what it is. It looks like a bag of weed to me, but I don't know where it came from. You probably put it there!"

That was not the smartest thing to say, though I honestly had no idea where the bag of weed came from, and I knew it was not mine. The officer immediately shoved me against the side of the truck and said, "Look here, punk, if I wanted to plant something, I'd plant something big enough to bury you." He then proceeded to place us under arrest for possession of marijuana and then read us our rights. (I learned later that another friend had borrowed a leather Army-surplus shell case of mine that past weekend when we were camping, and he had left a bag of weed in it. He also left it in my glove compartment.)

I started praying. I had turned seventeen a few weeks before, which meant I would not be charged as a juvenile but as an adult. And that meant I'd be brought to a hell hole of a jail known as Parish Prison, which served as both a parish jail (the term *parish* is equivalent to a county in most states) and a prison. There were three floors. The first was primarily devoted to reception, where new arrests were processed and held until they were bailed out or stood before a judge. If after three days they had not been bailed out, they would be moved to the second or third floor. This was definitely not where a skinny, seventeen-year-old wanted to find himself among seasoned detainees!

So, I prayed and kept praying, "God, *please* let Dad be out of town for work." I prayed that because, if my father were home, he would have said, "Let him spend a few days there and learn his lesson." It would not have been because he didn't love me, but tough love was his rule of thumb, and he practiced it to the T. When I was given the allotted one phone call, I discovered Dad was out of town. That was my first answer to prayer.

Unlike my father, my mother wasted no time doing what was necessary to get me bailed out. At the time, it required two property owners to sign for my release along with what-ever bond they had assessed for the charges. Bail was set at 10 percent of $1,000, making it $100. Mom asked our next-door neighbor, Nock, to accompany her to bail me out.

When the guard opened the cell door where Tony and I were kept, he called our names and announced we had been "bailed out." That was a major step in the right direction, as

I would escape the second or third floor. That was my second answer to prayer.

As we walked out of Parish Prison in downtown New Orleans, at somewhere around three that humid and muggy August morning, I remember thinking how lost I was, while at the same time thinking I just needed to get smarter if I was going to continue to live the life I seemed to have chosen to live. My head was swirling with so many emotions and thoughts I could not process them quickly enough. I was full of shame, embarrassment, guilt, and hurt for my mother whom I knew had never dreamed she would be bailing her son out of jail for any reason, much less for possession of an illegal substance.

While all these thoughts and fears and emotions were funneling through my mind and soul, all of a sudden something hit me in the seat of my pants that literally lifted me off the ground. Walking in front of my mother, my head bowed down under the load of shame and embarrassment, Nock decided a good kick in the seat of my pants would be the most appropriate attempted wake-up call I could use at the time! I did not even turn around to look at him. I merely accepted my due deserts and kept walking.

Nock's kick came at the perfect time, right in the middle of the tornado of thoughts and emotions churning inside me. I knew I couldn't turn around and contest his parental representation on my father's behalf in my father's absence, as well as his own sentiments about my stupidity and thoughtlessness, especially having just helped to bail me out. I had no ground to stand on, and my bearing offered no arguable position to oppose his very clear statement, "Get your act together, stupid, and don't drag your mother through another skit like this, or next time you will get to sit it out in jail and learn your lesson."

Lostness, there I was again. But this time, I was not as anxious to heed its alarms. I spent another year searching and sniffing like a dog the scent of other paths that were leading nowhere.

———

By the time I had turned eighteen and my brother, Jim, nineteen, we had decided that, if we could just get out of this place—out of New Orleans—maybe we would find what we were searching for. We both felt trapped in an unending cycle of futility, chasing our rebellious culture's appetites and trends, and going nowhere fast with no sense of purpose or direction. I felt like I was standing on the edge of a cliff, fighting against the wind that was about to push me over the edge. I knew something needed to change radically, or I was going to plummet to my very ruin.

I don't want to over- or under-dramatize those years, but for quite some time, there was no lack of inner confusion and frustration that helped to beg the question of our culture, "Does anybody have a clue what life is really all about?"

Looking back, the two bookends of the day that still stand out to me were the Vietnam War, with its looming draft of almost every male turning eighteen, and Woodstock. Both were reactions against conflicts, both multiethnic and societal, national and international. Consequently, we were challenging the status quo, and instead of walking "the straight and narrow" as our parents prepared us and expected us to do, we were succumbing to the downward spiral of a reactionary culture and influence while bordering life-controlling addictions whose chains were already rattling in our very souls.

Jim had been checking out what he called a charismatic Bible study, which at the time sounded more like a mystical séance to me. Having been raised in a traditional Roman Catholic environment, Dad was committed to keeping us in Catholic schools, feeling it to be more beneficial than the public system at the time. He valued the education, influence, and even more importantly, the discipline that would be offered there. I benefited from the consciousness of God that was developing inside me, but I learned more about rules than I did relationship, which only added to the frustration and increasing sense of lostness I was experiencing.

Though I had rebelled and left home a year earlier in an attempt to leverage my father's steeled determination to keep us in the private school environment, Jim was more compliant and resigned to get his diploma before exercising his rights to freedom. One of our instructors, a Jesuit brother who was our Spanish teacher, was orchestrating the Bible study that Jim was attending from time to time. To me, it seemed so contrary to the subculture of music, self-discovery, and drugs that accompanied these things that I could not comprehend how a Bible study could hold any answers for us. Soon enough, hunger for life's purpose and frustration with the same ruts of self-gratification and its cohorts convinced us both we could not get what we were looking for anywhere in New Orleans!

I'll never forget the day that Jim announced, "I'm going to find Jesus!" Just like that, he had proclaimed what we both knew in our hearts was the answer, though we really weren't sure if or how He could be found. Within days, Jim had pulled out of our seedy apartment in the ninth ward, dispersed his dozen and a half dogs (literally) that he had acquired in his misguided mission of mercy in the hood, and headed east to Florida. He did hold on to one dog, however, to share the journey with. Her name was Duck.

After three weeks had gone by, I decided Jim really had the best plan I had heard so far. Neither of us had given a single thought at the time to furthering our education, though we both had attended a reputable, college-prep high school and would likely have fared well had we been able to focus on school. But that was the problem. How could we focus on something like classes or earning a degree when our souls were burning to comprehend why God, if there really was a God, even put us here on the planet in the first place? The whole culture was screaming at the time, "Why are we here? Does life have any meaning? Why are so many of our peers being called to war on the other side of the globe?"

The Vietnam conflict had been raging for several years by then, provoking strong anti-war sentiments and demonstrations on college and university campuses across the country. There had been open flag burnings and other often riotous reactions to our government's decision to engage in a war that wasn't considered by many to be our own. The impact that drugs and substance abuse were having on the culture was immense as well, aided and abetted by a music culture that was seeding a generation with a philosophy of independence and rebellion, challenging the status-quo for its embedded ideas without substantive explanation for its ruling values. It really was a crazy time, and we were "coming of age" at the peak of it all.

After a few weeks had passed, I decided to track Jim down, anxious to see if he had made any progress in his search for Jesus. Initially, he had said he was headed east, so I made my way to the Gulf Coast of Florida and managed to locate where he had found a job with a framing contractor. Apparently, he had earned a couple hundred dollars, and he and Duck then headed west for California, as though drawn by a great magnetic pull in that direction. I was able to find a couple of guys who worked for the same crew Jim had found work with, and they pointed out where he had been camping the last couple of weeks.

Across Highway 90—the two-lane state highway that was sporting a massive growth of condominiums, townhouses, and beach houses—stood a billboard sign surrounded with tall, overgrown shrubbery. I walked across the road to survey the site, and sure enough, the grass was matted down as though a small tent had been pitched there. A place where a small fire had been built attested to the fact that someone had been residing beneath the makeshift shelter provided by the sign and shrubbery. I was intrigued how Jim had managed to spend so many days there without being asked to move on. He was gone, and I wondered if it was going to be possible to find him, now that he had headed toward the big West Coast.

———

By the time I caught up with Jim's trail in the San Francisco Bay area of California, specifically Berkley, at least six to eight weeks had lapsed, and he was already on his way back east to find me, his kid brother. Calling back east from Chinatown in San Francisco, I learned from my parents that Jim was anxious to see me and that he was expected to arrive there any day. I knew in my heart that he must have discovered something that he really wanted to share with me. Still ringing in my ears were his words, "I'm going to find Jesus!" Maybe in fact by now he had!

I decided not to hitchhike all the way across the country, so I boarded a Continental Trailways bus for the projected three-and-a-half-day trip to Atlanta. Our parents had moved that summer from New Orleans to Atlanta, and that's where Jim would be waiting for me. As painful as that ride back east was, it was my chance to read almost cover to cover the paperback edition of the New Testament I was carrying with me. It was called, *Good News for Modern Man*, courtesy of the Catholic Church.

On that sixty-seven-hour trek back home, I began to realize the one thing that had been tethering the kite of my wind-tossed life to the ground through those challenging years. It was a promise I had made when I was thirteen years old. Invited to a boy's camp sponsored by the Catholic Church, I had been sold on the fact that there was an Olympic-size pool, baseball, horseback riding, basketball, and much more in a beautiful country setting. As the week had progressed, I had realized it was a recruiting tool the church had used to interest young men in the priesthood (while they were young, and before they became too inter-ested in girls, which was already too late for me, but I was on board for the fun). By week's end, a Jesuit brother had given a talk that had emphasized the nature of a vow and how binding such a commitment was. The "vow" he had presented to us in closing his talk was a vow to read a chapter of the Gospels in the New Testament for an entire year before going to sleep every night. I had thought that certainly could not hurt, and I wasn't making a commitment to be a priest, so I had raised my hand and said, "I'm in!" As the year progressed, it wasn't easy to keep such a commitment, and no doubt I missed a day here and there. But what that year of reading one chapter of the Gospels every night had deposited in me was about to come alive in a way that my soul had been longing for since those earlier days.

When Jim and I finally caught up with each other back in Atlanta, I knew something significant had happened to him.

Chapter 3

"Hey, Bro, You Want the Real Deal?"

JIM AND DAD HAD DRIVEN TOGETHER TO THE BUS station in downtown Atlanta to pick me up. I remember distinctly recognizing the change in demeanor and disposition in Jim that led me to wonder what he had experienced. I couldn't wait to hear his story. That night, after arriving at the house, we sat down to catch up on the two months that had elapsed since we had been together.

Jim told me that he had found his way out to the Bay Area of San Francisco, where he encountered some people whom he thought would introduce him to Jesus. They spoke of Jesus and assured Jim that they could arrange for him to meet Jesus. The group called themselves the *Unification Church,* led by the Rev. Sun Myung Moon from Korea. Jim had already been among them for close to a week when they gave him the task of putting up advertisements for the meetings they were having in downtown Berkley. One afternoon, while stapling their flyers to telephone poles along the sidewalks in Berkley, a genuine Christian (a true follower of Jesus) came behind him and removed the flyers just as fast as Jim put them up!

Pausing to decide where he would go next, Jim looked back down the street where he noticed the guy tearing down the advertisements he had been stapling up. The young man was putting them in a garbage bag. Intrigued and a bit agitated at the same time by what he had just witnessed, Jim stepped into the alcove of a storefront and waited for the guy to come his way. When the young man got to where Jim was standing, Jim stepped out, with his full-length red hair (like the cover of the *Hair* album, if you remember the musical), and confronted him.

"What are you doing with my flyers?" Jim asked him.

"Man," he said, "this stuff is bogus! If you want the real deal, you need to come with me!"

Jim asked him, "Do you guys know Jesus?"

"You better believe it, we do! Come see for yourself!"

"Then let's go," Jim said.

His newfound friend replied, "Here, you won't need those flyers anymore," as he dropped the remainder of them in his bag and then into a public garbage can while he and Jim made their way up the street.

Jim followed the guy back to a ministry that was being led by a young minister named Mario Murillo, a fiery and passionate evangelist who possessed a great zeal for the lost, particularly for the hippie culture of the day. It was a genuine gospel-teaching and practicing ministry and community where Jim experienced a very genuine encounter with Jesus. Jim stayed on for a little less than two months and began his walk with God by engaging in studying the Bible and discipleship training on a daily basis.

After several weeks had transpired, Jim remembered our last minutes we had together before heading off in different directions. Jim told me that, in keeping with his end of the deal, he started his journey back east to reconnect with me and share with me that he had in fact found Jesus!

When I first saw Jim at the bus station, he displayed a definite warmth and joy that was not exactly the norm for him. That first evening together, as he shared what he had personally experienced with the Lord, I could see and even feel the deep conviction of encounter he was describing. I asked Jim what I had to do to encounter God as he so clearly and dramatically had himself.

"Honestly, it's very simple," he said, "because God has already been drawing you to Himself!"

Jim went on to explain how Holy Spirit was already working in my heart to reveal Jesus to me and to make Himself real to me. I began tearing up. (No, let me man up. I was crying, and I could not explain why I was!) Looking back, I felt like I was being found, with ten times the sense of relief and release from my lostness than I felt as a four-year-old explorer encountering the mailman who would take me home. I understood later that Holy Spirit had been drawing me all my life, but it was more pronounced in the couple years leading up to that moment.

Jim led me in a simple prayer to affirm that I wanted to know Jesus and what Jesus had done for me personally. Jim explained to me how sin separates us from God, just as it did with the very first man and woman when they chose what God had directed them to avoid. When Adam made that choice, his disobedience was sin, which marred his nature, and that marred nature was passed to all humanity, especially to me. Jesus came to accept our punishment for sin and impart God's very nature back to us, as we are born of His seed, making Him our Father. In that moment, I knew I was coming alive for the first time in my life. When I asked Jesus for forgiveness, I felt liberated from a fallen nature and all my thoughts, words, and deeds of a lost life.

To this day, I can still remember the overwhelming sense of love, acceptance, and forgiveness that I felt from God in that moment. I had never experienced anything like that before. A deep, profound, and exhilarating sense of God's love and presence embraced me and gripped me for several hours. It even continued for days after. I was awestruck with a sense of belonging, acceptance, and purpose, and for the very first time in my life, I felt a sense of identity and understanding of who I was and why I was on the earth! It would not be until sometime later that I would comprehend so much more of what was transpiring in those initial moments of connection with my Heavenly Father. What would being a son and a disciple of His really mean? All I knew at that moment was I could not wait to continue this journey with Father, Son, and Holy Spirit that had undeniably just begun.

Right away, Jim explained how important the Bible was. He said, without it, we really have no guide by which to know what God's plan for our lives is. I purposed to buy one the very next day. Jim and I made plans to visit a bookstore where he would show me a specific study Bible that he had become familiar with. (I really think he just wanted to borrow mine from me as often as possible!)

Chapter 4

Where Do We Go from Here?

IT WAS SATURDAY NIGHT, AND LESS THAN TWENTY-four hours earlier, I had experienced the encounter of a life-time and determined to follow Jesus and grow in my rela-tionship with Him. I was still soaring on the experience and had spent most of the day grilling Jim for more information on this astonishing encounter with God I had experienced the night before. We were driving home in the car with Dad that evening when Jim said suddenly, "Pull in here!"

Dad was driving, so he asked, "Where? Into this church driveway?"

"Please," Jim responded, and we pulled into the driveway of a church. The sign out front read, "Life & Praise Tabernacle." The sign had a dove painted on it with a tagline beneath the name which read, "A Christ-centered, Spirit-filled Fellowship." Jim asked Dad if he would give him a minute to check it out. Jim jumped out of the car, just as several men were coming out of the front doors of the church. He approached them, exchanged a few words with them, got back in the car, and said, "This is the place!"

I said, "What do you mean this is the place?"

Jim replied, "This is where we're going to church tomorrow!"

Upon our very first visit, we both knew this was where the Lord was planting us. We never even visited another church. We felt from the beginning that this was the place the Lord had intended for us to get plugged in and connected. Hungry to grow in this relationship with God, I unconsciously purposed to be in attendance every time the doors were opened and sometimes even when they weren't!

It was a warm, accepting fellowship of believers, with a pastor who took immediate interest in Jim and me, as though we were members of his own family. Honestly, church had never felt that way before to either of us. We were more accustomed to trying to avoid church than actually wanting to be there.

I found myself very eager to understand the Bible and to discover the wealth and treasure of wisdom and spiritual understanding Jim had explained it contained. I took as much time as possible to read, and I asked Jim as many questions as I could about what he had already learned from his time in the book.

Meanwhile, Jim was making plans to return to California where he had encountered the Lord. He explained that he had begun to be "discipled" and wanted to return for a period of time to continue growing in this dimension. Of course, it was all new to me, but I was intrigued to discover that the Lord could still be gathering and developing disciples just as He had when He had called that first twelve to "be with Him."[1]

By the time Jim was ready to leave, I was pretty well settled into the church, which was only two miles from our parents' home. I found a job on a construction crew on a referral from someone at the church, and my life consisted pretty much of work and reading the Word. Honestly, it was wonderful! I was yet to really grasp the concept of discipleship, though I was hearing the term mentioned here and there. I know now that Jim was returning to California to engage himself in a more formal commitment to discipleship as he had come to understand it in the short lifespan of his relationship with God.

---

1. Mark 3:14

Chapter 5

The Great Escape

ONE OF THE FIRST MOVIES THAT STUCK TO THE screen of my mind and memory as a youngster, besides *The Wizard of Oz*, was the classic *The Great Escape*. Though oftentimes I may not remember the starring actors' names, Steve McQueen has been an easy one to remember. The movie was derived from the real-life history surrounding the escape of British Commonwealth prisoners of war from a POW camp in Nazi Germany.

After months of digging tunnels under the camp's facilities, with the goal of emerging outside the barbwire fences, the escape was prematurely set in motion. When McQueen appeared above ground to discover that their tunnel had come short of clearing the fence, the guards detected their plot, and the scrambling to escape was then frantically in action. McQueen spotted a nearby motorcycle used by the guards, and the chase was on! McQueen's determination, though courageous and dramatic (he insisted on doing the stunt himself rather than using a professional stuntman), was foiled when he and the motorcycle were trapped in a row of rolled barbwire. Attempting to jump over to his freedom, his efforts were valiant and heroic but resulted in his return to the camp, then having to endure more severe punishment and abuse for his attempt to escape.

For me, having emerged from the tunnels of my soul's imprisonment and untangled from the barbwire fence and its relentless grip, I realized my escape had been an act of divine intervention in my life. I had repeatedly failed miserably in my own efforts to escape the dungeon of my lost existence, but now, somehow God had brought me into the most liberating experience of a lifetime. In the words of the notable hymn writer and revivalist, Charles Wesley, "My chains fell off, my heart was free, I rose went forth and followed Thee."[1]

During that first year of walking with the Lord, somehow Holy Spirit made a way for me to find myself in a lively spiritual atmosphere, immersed in a community of believers whose values and lifestyle were what I needed. Thankfully, I was five hundred miles from the culture and influences that had held their grip on me. While it was not an easy decision to make, moving on from relationships that are engulfed in the atmosphere of imprisonment and toxins to your soul and building connections with those with shared goals to grow in a relationship with God and His people are necessary if you are ever to retain true freedom and purpose in Christ. Continuing to pray and believe that God has your redemption and destiny in His hands is in order, but too often the continued connection with these compadres leads you back to the prison camp of old habits and negative thinking and *lostness*.

In addition to that, the dramatic contrast to the repetitive, religious, ceremonial environment that I had grown up in and had known church to be was an immediate and refreshing change. Every service I would attend held a new glimpse and insight of who God really was and what walking with Him meant. Unlike what I had been accustomed to, I was no longer counting the minutes until church was over, feeling I had paid my dues for the week till the next time I would have to return and endure the pain of another service. No, now I was leaving every service or gathering of any kind with tools for the journey that I couldn't wait to put into practice.

Another major discovery was experiencing the very *tangible presence of God.* I had been taught that God was omnipresent, which is true, of course, and encouraging to know. What I didn't know was God is very interested in allowing His people to actually experience His presence in a literal, "felt" way. I would soon learn that there would be those who would look at such a culture with skepticism and, even worse, cynicism. The Bible is full of accounts of both, but certainly cynicism reaches beyond the discomfort of skepticism to openly criticize and chide those whose faith has claimed for them an encounter with God yet to be known by the cynical disclaimers of what they merely cannot comprehend without faith. Because faith is a gift from God,[2] it is readily available to "whosoever will,"[3] and growing in faith was and still is a staple of the experiences and culture of the redeemed. I began to understand that Holy Spirit was working in my life, depositing His truth and understanding, not only when I was reading the Bible, but throughout my day, He was occupying my thinking with a continuing consciousness of God that I had not known before.

I was so hungry to understand more about this, that in addition to reading the Bible without limits, I would offer to help my pastor every chance I could get in order to spend time with him. My pastor spiritually took me under his wing, and before long, I realized he had become a real spiritual father and mentor to me.

As that first year rolled on, I found myself growing in ways I would never have thought possible. I began to sense a passionate tug in my heart to really know God and to serve Him any way I possibly could. Though I was growing and learning and experiencing spiritual growth immersed in the church community and culture, I thought maybe a more formal and committed approach to training for ministry might be in order. Then I came across a passage in Luke's Gospel that I remember misusing to serve my own interest while rebelling against my parents and other authority.

"If anyone comes to Me and does not hate his father and mother, wife and children, brothers and sisters, yes, and his own life also, he cannot be My disciple. And whoever does not bear his cross and come after Me cannot be My disciple."

— Luke 14:26–27

I knew the Lord was calling me, but He was letting me know that He was going to be the One to define what that meant and looked like. Digging beneath the surface of the word *hate* as is found in the English translations of the

Bible, I found that the original concept Jesus was communicating was "love less." Jesus certainly was not commanding us to hate our families in the sense that we know the word today, but He was commanding that we not place any love above that which belongs to Him. To "prefer" family above Himself was to lose sight of His place in us and to surrender His call to discipleship that's upon our lives.

One Sunday morning, not long after that, a visiting pastor addressed me directly in the middle of his message and said I was to begin to prepare for the call of God that was upon my life, and not to delay! I took that word seriously as from the Lord, and that spark ignited what was already churning inside me. I made it a point to talk with my pastor about that word first chance I had.

I wasn't aware of this, but my pastor was the son-in-law of the founders of a small, but influential Bible school in the Northeast.[4] Though he was familiar with several other schools and different training ministries, my pastor's relationship and loyalties were understandably with this school. He had not only attended the school, but had also developed a close relationship with its founder. At the time he attended, the school had a small farm that helped supply food for its faculty and students. Having grown up on a farm himself, my pastor was right at home helping with the daily chores of the farm. The founder also had been an experienced farmer and spent what time he could spare from his other duties to help the farm provide much needed food for the school. In this context, a discipling relationship developed between the founder and my pastor.[5] My pastor would eventually marry one of the founder's daughters. He told me during our conversation that, in just a few weeks, the vice president of this school would be visiting the church, and he would arrange for both my brother and me to meet with the vice president of the school.

The vice president came, and Jim and I met with him. After our meeting, both Jim and I felt it might be a good fit for both of us. We applied and, within a week or two, were accepted. We set the date on the calendar and began to prepare for our departure in late August of that year.

The closer that day came, for some reason, the less enthused I was about leaving. I really couldn't put my finger on why, but the excitement was waning by the day.

Then another minister visited the church, little more than a week before I was to depart for school in the Northeast. He was the president of a similar Bible school in Texas. He was visiting for two nights of ministry. Both nights, he spoke from the Gospels, specifically on the life of Christ. I was moved by his grasp and delivery of the life and ministry of Jesus, and my appetite for more had been awakened. I spoke with my pastor after the services and explained how my anticipation for leaving to attend school was waning, until now. I asked him, "What would you think about me applying to attend this man's school?"

He agreed it would probably be a good experience and made a statement I remember to this day. "God uses men...!" He naturally meant women as well but was referring to the fact that God places us in relationship with His people and uses them in our lives. It's simply how God works.

I asked the visiting minister if there was still enough time to process an application for the coming school year. He said there was. I wasted no time in getting it submitted, and within days, I received a letter of acceptance. I packed my bags and made the near thousand-mile drive to San Antonio only a few days later. There, I attended International Bible College (IBC)[6] to continue this unfolding encounter with the One who was continuing to draw me to Himself.

———

Note from publisher: We encourage you to read the endnotes that are associated with the text as they often provide valuable insight, biographical information, or additional details to enhance your reading experience.

1. The name of this Wesley hymn is "And Can It Be, That I Should Gain?" It was published in 1738 and is in the public domain.
2. "For by grace you have been saved through faith, and that not of yourselves; it is the gift of God, not of works, lest anyone should boast" (Ephesians 2:8–9).
3. "'The word of faith is near you, in your mouth and in your heart,' (that is, the word of faith which we preach); that if you confess with your mouth the Lord Jesus and believe in your heart that God has raised Him from the dead, you will be saved. For with the heart one believes unto righteousness, and with the mouth confession is made unto salvation. . . . For 'whoever calls on the name of the Lord shall be saved'" (Romans 10:8–10, 13).
4. Elim Bible Institute was founded by Ivan and Minnie Spencer in 1924. They opened the "training school" to train young men and women for last days' revival ministry. Ivan Q. Spencer's life of faith was chronicled in *Ivan Spencer: Willow in the Wind* by Marion Meloon. Two posthumous publications contain Ivan's thoughts on faith: *Faith: Living the Crucified Life* and *Daily Seedings: A Devotional Classic for the Spirit-filled Life.* My pastor was George Veach, and he had married one of the founders' daughters, Ruth Spencer.

5. Discipling relationships occur very organically spiritually. More will be addressed regarding this topic in a later chapter.

6. IBC was founded by a man named Leonard Coote, an Englishman who was a very successful businessman working in Japan when he encountered the Lord for the very first time. An admirer of ancient literature, he enjoyed reading the Bible when time permitted. He had read through the Scriptures several times, but when coming to Matthew 6:19–21, regarding accumulating treasure on Earth versus laying up treasure in heaven in the record of the Sermon on the Mount, he felt very uncomfortable because of his successful earnings and wealth. His practice was to skip that section when he would approach it until one day Holy Spirit compelled him to read through it carefully. It was on that occasion that he bowed his heart and knee to the lordship of Jesus Christ, and surrendered his life to Him, having had a genuine personal encounter with the living God whose very Word he had grown to value and appreciate as a work of literature. Not long after, he began a training institute in Icoma, Japan, called Icoma Bible College, to prepare workers for end-time harvest ministry. After the Second World War, in 1946, he came to the United States to found IBC in San Antonio to prepare harvest laborers for ministry in the Far East and around the world.

Chapter 6

He's Still Calling Disciples

THE THOUSAND MILES TO SAN ANTONIO WAS A
time of intense reflection, thinking about what this new
chapter was going to hold. Before Bible college was a
consideration for either of us, Jim had travelled back to
Berkley to be a part of a discipleship program that was
specifically directed toward our generation and culture. It
was not until Jim had been gone for a few weeks that I was
understanding more and more that *discipleship* was God's
design and intent for everyone born of Him and surrendered
to His plan for their lives.

Jim's passion for the Word was inspiring and motivating,
and I was realizing Holy Spirit was applying new disciplines
and restraints to Jim's daily life as a result of what he was
discovering in the Word. Our conversations then were often
reflections of things we were coming across in the Bible.
One day, while reading John's Gospel, I came upon how
Andrew introduced his brother, Peter, to Jesus. My heart
was warmed to know Jim and I had that in common with

47

Andrew and Peter. I will forever owe gratitude and respect to my brother for his being Andrew in my life.

But now I was driving west while he was headed north to attend the school we had originally considered together. I'm sure that was God's design, as we both would be plunged into distinctly new environments focused on encountering God and submerging ourselves in His Word.

Once I arrived at IBC in San Antonio, Texas, I continued to immerse myself in the Word but now with a measure of direction and guidance. I was fascinated with the life and work of Christ, and found that to be the most compelling of all the courses offered. It was during this season that I became even more enthralled with what Jesus taught about sonship and His relationship with His Father, as well as discipleship. I found that both concepts engage us in a relationship of love, trust, and obedience to our Father, and could be summarized by two specific sets of Christ's words: "Follow Me" and "Abide in Me."

It's interesting that many of the recorded exchanges between Jesus and Peter emphasized *discipleship*, while much of what John recorded of His teaching focused on *sonship*. I don't intend to try to dissect those two concepts but simply to stress their union and relationship for those who have been born from above. Peter described those who were *born of God* as those who were "begotten again, not of corruptible seed, but of incorruptible, through the word of God, which liveth and abideth."[1] The *new birth* is an authentic, definitive, and obvious spiritual experience initiated by God Himself with the person who through faith accepts Him as Father. Thus begins an eternal journey with Him that spans this life and crosses the divide between this world and the life to come. Peter's words differentiated between the perishable and imperishable, describing the *Word* of God as the very *seed* from which one has been born again, "which lives and abides forever!"

> "All flesh is as grass, and all the glory of man as the flower of the grass. The grass withers, and its flower falls away. But the word of the Lord endures forever."

— 1 Peter 1:24–25

---

1. 1 Peter 1:23 ASV

Chapter 7

The Carnal Disciple

IT WAS ALREADY SUMMER AFTER THE FIRST YEAR of focused study of the Bible and ministry training and experience at IBC. Standing on the steps outside chapel just a couple of months earlier, I had met (for the second time) a missionary to Mexico who was a living legend in that culture. That morning, only moments before, he had spoken in chapel. While exiting the building, he had noticed and recognized me from when he had visited Life & Praise Tabernacle in Georgia. He had spoken there before I had left for school.

In almost the same breath of reconnecting and greeting one another, he invited me to work with him that summer in Mexico in the ministry he was developing. He explained to me how he flew a small Cessna airplane over the rugged terrain of Mexico, dropping literature on remote villages, and how he would go back to those villages in a four-wheel-drive vehicle to begin the demanding task of reaching the villagers with the gospel and planting a church. In addition to that, a hundred-acre ranch and beautiful ranch house had just been donated to his ministry to start a much-needed orphanage in the region. Excited about the adventure of it all, I responded to his invitation by saying, "I will certainly pray about it," but my mind was already made up, my bag was packed, and I was well on my way!

I have to confess that I never even saw the plane that summer, though I know now that enticed me as much as (or more) than the purpose of the mission itself. Truth is I saw very little of the missionary as well! Instead, I spent roughly two months pruning a ninety-acre orchard of orange trees blighted by a rare freeze that had dipped down into northern Mexico the winter before. Additionally, I completed numerous other daily chores and repairs around the ranch house where the orphans lived. I worked through solid, full-throttle days for the eight weeks in over one-hundred-degree temperatures and humidity that topped the charts. It was not exactly what I had envisioned and unconsciously hoped the missions trip would involve. Along with the work in the orchard and daily maintenance of the property, I was asked to assist with their bee business, which was helping to subsidize expenses for the home.

One day, I was assisting the master bee worker to make divides. This involved introducing new queens to the population in order to make more bee columns, increasing population and honey production. I was encouraged to wear a couple pairs of pants and two long-sleeve shirts, and I would be provided with gloves and a safari-style hat with netting to protect myself from what would soon be very annoyed and aggressive bees as their colony was about to be disturbed.

As I lifted a section of the wooden boxes that housed the bees, I was immediately swarmed by hundreds of bees, covering my gloves, shirts, and pants, as well as bees bombarding the well-worn netting that hung from the brow of my hat and covered my face. I had already been stung a few times through my shirts and pants, which I was tolerating, but then I suddenly realized there were three or four bees that had found their way inside the netting meant to protect my face from such invaders. While holding the boxes I had lifted from the columns—bees diving and landing on my hands, arms, face, and chest—I realized I had some newly found *compañeros* introducing themselves up close and personal. No sooner had I realized they were on the inside of the netting than they began to march between my nose and top lip, and decided in unison to send a clear signal, "Leave us alone, Gringo!"

Immediately, in unison, I could almost hear them count, *"Uno, dos, tres . . ."* when one after the other they drove their stingers into my face above my upper lip! Somehow, I managed not to scream like a Girl Scout, but calmly and very intentionally, I told the bee master, "Excuse me, but I have to set this box down for a minute, and I'll be right back!"

I proceeded to place the box back on the column and ran as fast as my legs could carry me, swatting off bees as I ran, looking for a safe place to escape the swarm that was following me. There was a nearby block building used to house tools and equipment that had an open window about four feet off the ground. I decided I would dive through the window to escape the swarming bees and swat off any stragglers that remained.

As I made my launch through the window, the brow of the safari hat I was wearing blinded me from seeing the concrete header over the opening, and *bam*, my head (thankfully, inside the helmet) hit the header, and my body followed, landing inside the shed.

I sat on the ground with my body writhing in pain, and I began to assess my condition while the many signals of hurt were piercing my brain's circuitry from all over my body. Blood was dripping from my forehead and running down my face from where the metal brim of the safari-style hat had cut into my head as I had smashed into the cement header. Sitting there in a pile of hurt, I could still hear my three Mexican compadres, whom I would come to call *Los Tres Amigos*, buzzing and looking for an exit light to find their way back home. Other bees had also found access inside my clothes and were looking for their way out. But the wound on my forehead from slamming into the concrete header was commanding the most attention.

It was then that I knew God was speaking to me. No, it was not audible, but it was louder and more specific than spoken words could have delivered. I heard the Lord speak to me as clearly as I had ever heard His voice till then, as He said, "Whose idea was this—yours or Mine?"

Those words echoed through my spirit and being. Tears began to fall from my eyes, now mixing with the blood coming from the wound on my forehead. With a swirling fusion of spiritual emotions, I could feel the embrace of Father's love and correction simultaneously. I realized, as well, He had probably been offering this lesson in easier ways at earlier times, but apparently, I hadn't received what He had been endeavoring to communicate with me. Now was the time, and with a sense of lostness setting in, I confessed that I had followed my own desires, initiative, and directives, and not what I had received from Him.

On the way up to my room that night to collect the few hours of sleep that I would get before the first of the thirteen orphaned children would awaken and begin the day, I was told that I had received a letter in the mail. It was sitting on a desk at the bottom of the stairs, one of the few pieces of mail I can recall that I had received during the two months I was there. It was a letter from my pastor back in Georgia. He had taken the time to write and check in on me, expressing a concern that he was carrying for me at the same time. I will never forget the words that awaited me on that page.

After the usual greeting and opening lines, I read, "Son, it greatly disappointed me when you made your going to Mexico an announcement rather than, 'Pastor, what do you think?'"

Wow! Where did that come from? I was confused for a moment, and defensive thoughts flooded into my mind. But then Holy Spirit, the One who Jesus said would "guide [us] into all truth"[1] had the last say. I began to realize what my pastor was talking about. *How had I so quickly gotten to the place where his opinion on a decision and commitment like that was no longer important enough to pursue him for his input and counsel?*

I remember thinking about how much that felt like the comment of a father, which admittedly would cause me to protect my independence as though it were being threatened. But this time it was coming from a spiritual father who could see that, though I might be growing in knowledge of the Word and acquiring ministry experience serving in Mexico, like the Corinthians of old, I was regressing to a carnal state of immaturity, and avoiding an essential relationship of accountability—such accountability being characteristic of a mature follower and disciple of Jesus.

I remember lifting my eyes from the letter, spotted with tears of remorse and repentance, asking Father to forgive me for reverting to the independent spirit that had crept into my soul and relationship with my own earthly father from a young age. I was startled by this awakening and grieved that, even as a believer and a follower of Jesus, I could still be as unconsciously independent and chart a course for myself without the indispensable navigational tools of divine wisdom Father wants to dispense through relationship with God-appointed counsel. I determined I would visit my pastor upon my return home to restore the connection and vital flow of communication that I had allowed to dissolve through my pursuit of knowledge and experience.

This story introduces a dimension of discipleship that gradually dawned on me years later. The specific lesson of this story was not fully realized and certainly not completed then. The lesson would continue into the very next year. But what it helped me to see was the positive and negative sides of the coin of what we might call *carnal discipleship*.[2] Our translation of the word *carnal* from the original language of the New Testament is simply *immature* or not fully developed.

My pastor carried a God-given concern for me, as he did for his entire flock, and had sown into our lives (my brother's and mine) during that first year of our walks with God. But now, after a year of acquiring knowledge, I seemed to be losing the need for pastoral input and counsel. Instead, my focus was knowledge, experience, and developing skills for ministry. And with eyes wide open, I was slowly beginning to lose my way and revisit a new territory of lostness.

It happens. And I am not alone in this experience. It happens every day and is happening to young and old believers all around the world, especially where misguided values of success and a reframed image of God and His nature are exchanged for the surrender of our ambition to the cross of discipleship and the personal call and design of God for our lives.

In our Western society, we seem to associate acquiring knowledge and developing skills with maturity. But Paul told these same Corinthians believers, "Knowledge puffs up, but love edifies."[3]

The culture of training and equipping I was in placed a high value upon sacrifice and service to reach the lost, wherever they may be found. The rewards of acknowledgment and recognition were bestowed generously upon those who had achieved what was considered success, evidenced by numbers of conversions or people attending their churches, or the erection of facilities to house the ministries they had developed. So, when I was asked by a living legend of a missionary to join his team for a summer of ministry and experience, it fit what was becoming my understanding of success, maturity, and even God's expectation of me, and I didn't think for a moment of the pre-existing relationships that He had used to get me to where I was.

———

Carnal discipleship, is it a possible oxymoron? The definition of an oxymoron is "a figure of speech containing words that seem to contradict each other. It's often referred to as a contradiction of terms."[4] I say that because the first dimension of discipleship we want to identify is what we might surprisingly refer to as the *carnal disciple*. This youthful disciple, or what can eventually evolve into a casual-follower phase, is referred to in Paul's first letter to the Corinthians.[5] Paul was addressing the Corinthian believers, his own spiritual sons and daughters in the Faith, and referred to them as *carnal*. This can mean *not yet mature, as well as fleshly*.

Paul told his spiritual kids that he had wanted to speak to them as *spiritual people*, but he could not because they were still carnal, or immature, "behaving like mere men."[6] He said he wanted to feed them with *(spiritual)* meat, but they were not yet ready for it, because they were still accustomed to milk. In its initial positive stage, the carnal disciple is merely a young disciple; he or she is a newborn believer, making this season and dimension a very positive place to be. In Corinth, at the time, thankfully, there were many such believers. I would imagine they made up the lion's share of the church at the time of Paul's first letter to them. But he was also well aware that it was high time they became serious about growing up!

The visible symptoms of their condition, indicating their need to mature, was evident in their relationships with one another. The truth is we can examine ourselves and evaluate our relationships with God by how we choose to relate with one another. Early in this letter, Paul focused on the competitive nature of the Corinthians coming out in their preferences of teachers. And he later rebuked them for their self-centeredness, disclosed even in the practice of communion together. He wrote, "For when one says, 'I am of Paul,' and another, 'I am of Apollos,' are you not carnal?"[7] Paul also said,

> Now in giving these instructions I do not praise you, since you come together not for the better but for the worse. For first of all, when you come together as a church, I hear that there are divisions among you, and in part I believe it.
>
> — 1 Corinthians 11:17–18

The big picture here was *their prolonged and immature state was being displayed in their relationships.*

A real encounter with God, that results in accepting His redemptive pass at the supreme cost of His Son's sacrifice for us on the cross, opens the door to sonship with God and a relationship with our Heavenly Father for this life and the life to come. Almost immediately, your personal relationships display the reality or pretense of such an encounter with God.

When Paul cited the immaturity of favoritism in the Corinthians' relationships with one another, and their "following" favored teachers, they were manifesting a level of unhealthy immaturity and their prolonged stay in a carnal dimension of discipleship. The arrogance of knowledge was blinding them to the greater attribute of love, which he so well defined later in this same letter.[8]

In the same way that we all pass through childhood en route to further phases of development in life, the carnal disciple phase is an unavoidable passage for any Christ follower. When we experience the new birth, it is exactly that—a birth—which means we are starting at the fledgling phase and by design are moving toward full maturity. Like infancy and adolescence, it is a necessary season in our lives through which we must all pass. Though I didn't realize it at the time, I was moving through some of those phases myself.

At birth, we are totally dependent upon our parents or another caregiver to feed us, care for us, and help us develop the necessary skills to eventually feed ourselves. We had nothing to do with our entrance into this world, and similarly other than accepting God's free gift of new life in His Son, we have absolutely nothing to do with how that takes place as well. As Paul said,

Who then is Paul, and who is Apollos, but ministers through whom you believed, as the Lord gave to each one? I planted, Apollos watered, but God gave the increase. So then neither he who plants is anything, nor he who waters, but God who gives the increase.

— 1 Corinthians 3:5–7

Mature believers are not only unceasingly thankful to God for apprehending them and revealing Himself to them, but they humbly recognize their personal contribution to their new reality was merely *acknowledging their lostness* and accepting His redeeming and transforming love.

So, Paul further added, "Now he who plants and he who waters are one, and each one will receive his own reward according to his own labor."[9] This addresses our relationship with one another moving forward and our humble but significant place in building upon Christ's foundation in our lives and the lives of those around us.

Paul then said,

> For we are God's fellow workers; you are God's field, you are God's building. . . . For no other foundation can anyone lay than that which is laid, which is Jesus Christ.
>
> — 1 Corinthians 3:9, 11

This dimension is foundational, and as such is critical to our ongoing development in relationship to God and His children. Building upon the foundation He has laid is every believer's opportunity and responsibility to emerge from the tomb of a lifeless past into a life of genuine fruitfulness and usefulness to God. Paul used two illustrations, a field and a building, to describe God's work in us.

As a field, we are to produce fruit from the good seed He has and will continue to sow in us. As a building, we provide a habitation of God by His Spirit, which Paul reiterated by saying, "Do you not know that you are the temple of God and that the Spirit of God dwells in you?"[10]

The writer to the Hebrew believers also brought to light their responsibility to continue to grow as children of God and to accept that responsibility. Father's design is to entrust to each of us *relational responsibility and accountability* that come with growth.

By this time you ought to be teachers yourselves, yet here I find you need someone to sit down with you, and go over the basics on God again, starting from square one—baby's milk, when you should have been on solid food long ago! Milk is for beginners, inexperienced in God's ways; solid food is for the mature, who have some practice in telling right from wrong. So come on, let's leave the preschool finger-painting exercises on Christ and get on with the grand work of art. Grow up in Christ!

— Hebrews 5:12–6:1 MSG

Even though this concept may be easy to understand, it is not always so easily grasped. Being a *carnal disciple* becomes a negative thing after we have worn out our welcome in the nursery and its youthful stage, and we have not continued to mature, particularly *relationally*. It seems that, in Paul's day (and no doubt in ours as well), there were many such believers who were content to remain in the carnal phase and had yet to move forward and continue to mature. This is precisely what Paul was addressing when he wrote to the Corinthian church and challenged them, essentially saying it was time they put away their "training wheels"! He told them in 1 Corinthians 3:1–2,

And I, brethren, could not speak to you as to spiritual [mature] people, but as to carnal, as to babes in Christ. I fed you with milk and not with solid food; for until now you were not able to receive it, and even now you are still not able; for *you are still carnal*.

The word *still* implies that, while it might have been good for a while, Paul was suggesting that season should be behind them by now. It was high time for some growth and some fruit-bearing to be taking place in their lives.

Anyone who has worked with people in any capacity finds out soon that the level of their maturity is not measured merely by their knowledge of the subject or the mission, but by their ability and willingness to relate civilly and maturely to the rest of the community.

I wish I could say that first journey to Mexico was the end of the carnal disciple dimension for me. I have to admit, however, that it was not. In the course of the very next year, it took another more dramatic confrontation to bring it home. Only then did I grasp its reality in my life. Among the many spoken things that I learned from this process, there were several unspoken truths that continue to emerge to this very day as Father's process of change continues to work in my life.[11]

---

1. John 16:13
2. Paul used the term carnal four times in four verses, addressing his Corinthian children in the Faith (1 Corinthians 3:1–4). The Greek term is *sarkikos,* and it essentially means pertaining to the flesh. It refers to what is temporal, bodily, animal, and unregenerate. This is a strong term as it relates to those who should be developed, and it is more understandable relating to those newborn infants in their relationship with the Lord.
3. 1 Corinthians 8:1b
4. Definition taken from YourDictionary.com/.
5. 1 Corinthians 3:1–4
6. 1 Corinthians 3:3
7. 1 Corinthians 3:4

8. So much of Paul's letter to his Corinthian children in the Faith (and subsequently to us) was directed at their priorities and aligning them with the greater commandment of love that Jesus demonstrated and modeled while walking on the earth. Jesus said, "A new commandment I give to you, that you love one another; AS I HAVE LOVED YOU, that you also love one another. By this all will know that you are My disciples, if you have love for one another" (John 13:34–35). Paul, inspired by the Holy Spirit, highlighted the possession and use of spiritual gifts without love are of no value at all (see 1 Corinthians 13:1–13).

9. 1 Corinthians 3:8

10. 1 Corinthians 3:16

11. It can be expected that we all will recognize along the way the need to "grow up" in a given area of our lives, where maybe development of a specific attribute has been neglected for one reason or another. Paul's letter to the Romans clearly defines why God works "all things . . . together for good to those who love God, to those who are the called according to His purpose" (Romans 8:28). Paul explained God's purpose immediately after, saying, "For whom He foreknew, He also predestined to be conformed to the image of His Son, that He might be the firstborn among many brethren" (Romans 8:29).

Chapter 8

It's Not Over

ALMOST TO THE DATE, A YEAR LATER AFTER THAT initial invitation to go to Mexico, I was invited by the president of the school I was attending (IBC) to be one of three students he asked to travel that summer and represent the school, ministering in youth camps, local churches, and camp meetings all across the country. Once again, the invitation was so compelling that, though I said I would certainly pray about it, I was already on the road, driving mile after mile, preaching in youth camps and to youth groups in local churches, bringing students back with me to school that coming fall!

At the end of that summer and thousands of miles later, I made it home with just a couple of days to spare before school would begin again. The phone rang at my parents' home, and it was my pastor, asking if we could connect before I had to leave. I told him I would love to, and that I'd be leaving Saturday morning. It was Thursday. I agreed to meet him at his office the next morning.

That Friday morning, I was completely oblivious to what was about to happen. I was preparing to leave first thing Saturday for the thousand-mile road trip back to San Antonio, and a quick visit with my pastor was just one of the many to-dos on the list. I arrived at 9 a.m. as we had agreed. I walked into the foyer of the church, turned the corner, and walked down the hall that led to my pastor's office. I stepped through the office doorway, and there he was, rising from his desk to greet me with his usual open and affectionate spirit, embracing me like a son he hadn't seen since last Christmas! He asked me to sit down, and we exchanged brief stories of how things were going in our lives.

Then, he made this statement: "Son, I'm very concerned for you."

I thought, *Concerned for me?* I wondered what his concern could have been and began to compare inwardly my present state with my past before encountering the Lord. I thought, *You should've known me a couple of years ago; then you would really have had reason for concern! I've just returned from a summer tour of ministry, having recruited nearly a dozen students to join me at the school I'm attending, and you're concerned for me?* So, I said, "What are you concerned about?"

"My concern is I think you have come to a place in your walk with the Lord where you would rather speak than listen."

I was a bit dumfounded. I scooted forward in my chair, preparing to defend myself if necessary. I thought to myself, *Really? Where did this come from?* I braced for what was apparently going to be a confrontation with a man I deeply respected, but who somehow had the wrong perception of me and what I was about.

His next words were what I was not prepared for, and though they were simple in their expression, they were not his but sent from the Lord Himself: "Look at you." Three words, that's all he said, "Look . . . at . . . you."

In that moment, Holy Spirit was allowing me to see what I would never have seen without Him opening the eyes of my heart. And what He showed me startled me to the very core. Only moments earlier, I had no awareness that the course I was on was anything but what God had designed and assigned me to. But now I sat there thinking to myself, *How did I get so far afield from simply pursuing and following Jesus to find myself so far out on this narrowing branch in the quest for ministry instead?*

I remember feeling a sense of shock, even horror, in that moment. Though I knew I was undeniably free from the former vices and temptations that too often interfere and war against our relationships with God, the sense of being lost and even estranged from God was no less real in that instant. I dropped my head into my hands and began to weep. Holy Spirit was letting me see the already embedded roots of a misguided concept of ministry and its subtle derailing intent. My eyes were open to see the path I was on was one of my choosing, not the one Father had intended in His design and purpose for my life.

Almost immediately afterward, I kept finding confirming scripture for what I had experienced and where I had wandered off the trail. Jesus threw down some basic essential concepts in His Sermon on the Mount, found in Matthew 5–7 and Luke 10–11. In Matthew 7, He challenges us with the fact that not everyone who says to Me Lord, Lord will enter the kingdom of heaven, but he who does the will of My Father in heaven. Many will say to Me in that day, "Lord, Lord, have we not prophesied in Your name, cast out demons in Your name, and done many wonders in Your name?" And then I will declare to them, "I never knew you; depart from Me, you who practice iniquity."

— Matthew 7:21–23

It's arresting to find that the word *iniquity* is what Isaiah the prophet used to describe the willfulness and waywardness of us all when he says, "All we like sheep have gone astray; we have turned, every one to his own way; and the Lord has laid on Him the *iniquity* of us all."[1] *Iniquity,* simply put, is our going our own way, doing our own thing, even when we consider it a good thing to be doing, even spiritual! But it's not difficult to see that, when we begin to acquire some knowledge *about* God, the natural tendency will be to want to propagate what we've filled our heads with while our hearts could be adrift from the essential *life* that comes from closeness with Him.

Paul reminded the young Corinthian community of believers that "knowledge [alone] makes [people self-righteously] arrogant, but love [that unselfishly seeks the best for others] builds up *and* encourages others to grow [in wisdom]."[2] And J. B. Phillips in his New Testament translation of this same verse used these words to break down even further the passage and concept: "We should remember that while knowledge may make a man look big, it is only love that can make him grow to his full stature."

It has become apparent to me that the further along we go in this journey, from both personal experience and what I've observed over the years, there are many who minister out of the barrenness of intimacy and its ensuing life, driven by the image and coveted success factors of ministry. These are unconscious of the substitution that has been made by echoing the Word, rather than emulating and imparting *The Word Himself.*

When Paul was preparing to depart Ephesus, where he had spent the most amount of time in the course of his three distinct missionary journeys, torn with emotion over the bond that had been formed between him and the saints there, he made this comment, "So now, brethren I commend you to God and to the word of His grace, which is able to build you up and give you an inheritance among all those who are sanctified."[3] Paul first commended them to God, personally and intimately, to be joined with God and to abide in Him. And then, he commended them to the Word of His grace, as though the two (His Person and His Word) were on the same level. He said these together are "able to build you up"!

It is clear that God reveals Himself to us through His Word and continues to build us up in our relationship with Him as we abide in His Word and allow His Word to abide in us. But when the Word becomes an instrument of knowledge (*about* God) alone, we fall prey to the consequences of the fall of man. When Adam's eyes were opened to believe he had the capacity to discern good from evil, its consequence was the loss of absolute dependence upon God— upon the One who had created Adam for relationship and intimacy with Himself.

1. Isaiah 53:6
2. 1 Corinthians 8:1 AMP
3. Acts 20:32

Chapter 9

The Sojourn of Discipleship

As I wiped tears from my eyes, I asked my pastor straight out, "What do you think I should do?" I had already made more than enough decisions on my own. And I had failed to utilize an essential directional tool in my first two years of discipleship development and involvement in ministry. I had neglected the opportunity to ask the question that acknowledges the spiritual covering that these words reveal, "What do you think?"

Finally, I was willing not only to ask my pastor what he thought about what I had been thinking and already planning, but I was willing to ask him what he thought I should do.

Somewhat surprised by my response, my pastor answered, "It's not mine to tell you what to do. It is my place, however, to share with you what I think about what you're considering and help you weigh the pros and cons. Then you take that counsel and advice to prayer, and ask the Lord what you should do!"

That made perfect sense, offering me a practical yet biblical concept of both counsel and covering. My mind was still swirling in the amazement of how I missed this simple idea and vital compass, but I was determined not to lose the opportunity to use it now! I asked him what he thought about me considering transferring to Elim Bible Institute, the school that he had recommended initially, the one he had attended, and the one whose founder was his father-in-law. My pastor responded by saying, if I was open to that, he could look into it and see if my attending was still possible at this late notice.

Saturday morning, the very next day, I was driving north, headed to Elim instead of returning to IBC. That was not an easy decision, particularly after I had been recruiting students for IBC most of that summer, not to mention I was leaving behind the many relationships I had developed while there. But I had a sense of peace and resolve that this was the course the Lord had planned and designed.

As I made my way north, I reflected over and over on the relationships I would not be able to maintain, at least not in the same capacity. I was about to begin a whole new chapter without the sense of footing I had developed those past two years. I would be arriving at a place as the newcomer, completing the last year of the school's three-year program, and finding my way in a whole new culture. But my heart was open in a way I had not felt before, particularly to what internal change and likely course correction awaited me. I reflected on how I had often rejected my father's correction or suggestions about decisions I was considering. I was realizing I had adopted an independence that I would later learn was connected to what many would call an "orphan spirit." I would later come upon what Jesus would say to His disciples, "I will not leave you orphans: I will come to you."[1]

That year of school and training would in fact be a year of adjustment and discipline. Because I was arriving the last year of their three-year program, I was a stranger to those who had already developed friendships for the past two years. I accepted that as part of the road the Lord had designed for me to travel instead of returning to a school with the comfort of being an upperclassman and with the pride of having represented the school and influenced several new students to choose that school.

One of those disciplines that I encountered early on had to do with what were called "outstations." These were ministry assignments which all students participated in on a weekly basis, in addition to classes and any part-time jobs one might be engaged in.

I had hoped that, wherever I would be assigned, I would be able to work with Latins. I was feeling a sense of calling to return to Mexico or any Latin American country the Lord might choose to send me. I could not yet emphatically say, "I'm called to do or be this or that," but I was weighing and praying about this, and thought being able to continue to serve in a Latin community of some nature would be helpful with that.

When the initial assignments were posted on the Student Ministry board, I found my name on a team that would be going down to Montour Falls, a little town about 75 miles southeast of the school, to conduct Sunday services for a handful of elderly people. When we filled out the Student Ministry information form, it asked if we played an instrument or had a vehicle we could drive to the outstation. When I saw my name posted as the captain of the team, the driver, and the worship leader (because I played the guitar), I thought to myself, *Maybe this is the only criteria for this assignment.*

After returning very late from the church that first Sunday we went to Montour Falls, the next morning I visited the Student Ministry office and asked if I could speak with the director. I explained my interest in serving the Latin community and asked if he had seen my explanation of that on my information form. He simply told me the assignments had already been posted on the board, I could find where I had been assigned there, and there would be no changes. With only a thread of hope, I left his office and went straight to the Student Ministry board. Sure enough, my name was still posted on the Montour Falls assignment. Discipline had begun.

The three other students and I made the most of the assignment. We met at 7 a.m. every Sunday morning in the Elim courtyard and prayed together before leaving to get to the church by 9 a.m. The seventy-five-mile drive traversed the beautiful terrain of the Finger Lake region along the west side of Seneca Lake. We would conduct Sunday school for only three or four people at times, and now and then we would have a couple of children to share Bible stories with. After the morning service, we would generally visit Watkins Glen, hiking the rocky gorge that gave the town its name. The rock was carved through centuries of water flow and was, like all the eleven Finger Lakes in the region, the very "fingerprint" of the Flood that had left its signature around the globe.[2] Sometimes we would be invited to lunch at one of the elderly couples' homes, or to a single elderly woman's

trailer for some very old-school cooking, including dande-
lion greens and the like! When we had a chance, we would
work on homework if possible.

Then one Sunday, the pastor, who was planning on relo-
cating to North Carolina, where he was originally from,
invited us to have lunch at his home. After lunch, he asked
if he could meet with us. We sat in a small bedroom in his
mobile home dedicated to his office while he asked us to
prayerfully consider which of us might be willing to return
after graduation to serve as the pastor. Thankfully, I
thought, I had already been planning on spending two
months in Baja California, just outside of La Paz, to fulfill
my senior internship.[3] I thought for sure that, during those
couple of months, another student would be assigned to my
role, and upon my return to school, I would finish out the
year serving in a Latin church in the Rochester area.

As the Lord would have it, He had other things in mind!
Just before leaving campus to return home for a brief
Christmas visit with my family, before flying down to
Mexico to serve the two-month internship, I was called to
the vice-president's office to review my status for graduation. As I mentioned earlier, I transferred to Elim from IBC
with the understanding that my two years at IBC had transferred into EBI's three-year program for ministry and that I
would be graduating at the end of that third year. What I
was about to discover was that I would still need an additional eighteen units of study to complete their three-year
program, and those eighteen units would have to be spread
over two semesters. For just a moment, I thought I had been
misled, but just as quickly as that thought raced through my
head, I knew in my heart this was God's plan and design. I

wasn't sure in the moment how it was to play out, but it wouldn't be long before I would know.

———

I will never forget my return to campus after those two months that early winter in Mexico. Back home, we had heard that the Northeast was getting a lot of snow, and to this day, the winter of 1977 holds some records for snowfall and ice storms! Just before nightfall, I arrived on Elim's campus. It was a Sunday, late in February, and the campus was buried in snow. As I walked up the sidewalk bordered with snowbanks four to five feet tall toward what was known as the Admin Building, I saw a woman hurrying across the porch in the cold, heading toward the nearest entrance to the building. Then I heard the voice of the assistant to the director of Student Ministries call out my name.

"Hey, Jeff, welcome back! Those folks in Montour Falls are hoping you'll be coming back soon!"

That was all she had to say, and then she opened the door to the building and disappeared up the stairs.

That was not the greeting I would have expected, if I had expected anything! But now my mind was racing, building its reasoning why returning to Montour Falls was not the best idea for me, or them! Then I remembered what I had intended to do in the first place when the pastor presented us with the invitation for one of us to return and pastor the church. I decided I would go speak with the director of what was called the Home Missions Department of Elim Fellowship, the credentialing organization that was birthed out of the school to license and ordain its students as they became involved in ministry, both domestically and overseas. Surely the director would understand the church's need and recognize my youth and want to refer the church to someone with more ministry experience under their belt.

First thing that Monday morning, I called their office and made an appointment. The director could see me later that morning. After my first class, I headed down to his office. As I sat in front of his desk, I painted the picture of the past semester's ministry and experience with the handful of dear elderly saints our team had the privilege of spending our Sundays with. I explained how the pastor had asked one of us to seriously consider pastoring the church, as he was ready to retire. By this time, he had already moved to North Carolina, and the church was without a pastor. The student ministry team was holding the fort in the meantime, but when school was out in the spring, the church in Montour Falls would be completely without anyone to be with them.

I felt pretty confident he had the full picture of the need there, and his response would be something like, "Thanks, Jeff, for coming in and sharing the need with us. We'll review our list of available candidates and take care of it."

But that was not what he said. To my dismay, he said, "Now, Jeff, I understand you're a carpenter, is that right?"

"Yes, sir, that's right," I responded.

Then he said, "You're a man of the Word, aren't you?"

"Yes sir, I'd like to believe so."

"I think what the church needs is a Nehemiah, and you are a Nehemiah!" he concluded.

Though I must confess I really did not want to hear that, I knew his words were from the Lord. All my personal ambition was draining out of me as I sat and listened to what he had to say. He took the very same colors I had painted my picture with and continued to paint what He could see the Lord wanted to do if I could bring myself to see it! The truth was I was in sync with him, if not ahead of him, finding his words to be an anchoring confirmation of what I deeply sensed in my spirit. I could recognize not only the purpose and calling, but the Lord's divine safety, security, and continued disciplines which I had come to expect and accept. And I was sensing vividly that I was not only being protected from the next season of *lostness*, but was also receiving the tools to navigate the course of His design and not my own.

I recognized the additional year at school was part of His plan, though just how that would take shape was not then evident. The sting was not going away as quickly as I had hoped, realizing that if I were to make a commitment to the church, I would have to commute from there to school or from school to the church. Either way, a 150-mile (round-trip) commute was inescapable. But once again, I sensed God was in it, and I knew He would cover the bases.

I was finding a lot of comfort, understanding more and more what Job meant when he wrote:

"Behold, happy is the man whom God corrects; therefore do not despise the chastening of the Almighty. For He bruises, but He binds up; He wounds, but His hands make whole."

— Job 5:17–18

I would find that same encouragement in Proverbs, where Solomon penned:

> My son, do not despise the chastening of the Lord, nor detest His correction; for whom the Lord loves He corrects, just as a father the son in whom he delights.

> — Proverbs 3:11–12

And as if these encouragements were not enough, I found the writer to the Hebrews also drew from Proverbs and added this truth:

> If you endure chastening, God deals with you as with sons; for what son is there whom a father does not chasten? But if you are without chastening, of which all have become partakers, then you are illegitimate, and not sons.

> — Hebrews 12:7–8

Before learning that I would need another year to finish Elim's three-year program, the yearbook for that year was being assembled. Having come to a place of finding comfort and resolve in the disciplines and correction of the Lord, I began to think that I might use one of the above verses as my senior Scripture text that would be referenced in the yearbook. So, when the yearbook staff sent a young woman around to collect our verses, I decided I would use Job's reference and gave her Job 5:17 to accompany my senior picture in the yearbook. The day the yearbooks were handed out, I walked into the dorm, and the RA (resident advisor) on that floor heard my voice, and cried out, "Clark, what kind of verse is this?" referring of course to the scriptural text under my picture.

"What's wrong with it?" I replied. "It's a great passage, and in many ways, it's what this season in my life has been about!"

Holding his copy of the yearbook in his hand, he said, "Have you read this verse?"

"Why? What does it say?" I began to get a little concerned that maybe something had gone wrong! I spoke up and said, "It's Job 5:17, right?"

"No, it's Job 17:5!" he retorted. He began to read Job 17:5, not Job 5:17.

As he read the passage, my ears began to ring, and my mind began to spin! I couldn't stop the wave of thoughts flooding my consciousness, imagining the dismay and wonder anyone who read the verse would have as they reflected on what I was communicating. I thought for a moment that maybe it could be corrected, but knew if it could not, it would be what it was. And what it was was another discipline, and I knew it! The words he read were still pounding in my ears, "He who speaks flattery to his friends, even the eyes of his children will fail."

I was sure then, and undeniably am now, that there was some wisdom in that passage I could benefit from. But in that moment, I felt like trying to gather up all the yearbooks and somehow remove what everyone who read that verse both then and through the years would wonder. And then I felt the Lord whisper quietly yet profoundly to me, "Son, there's no need to boast in My correction; it's simply between you and Me!"

That season of coming into an understanding of my identity in Him, my sonship to Him—and renewing my surrender to His design, His plans, and His purpose—was in fact a reawakening period of my life. Yes, I thought, it would be appropriate to share what that season was about, but to the Lord, I learned it was more personal, and He wanted it to be such to me.

I quickly accepted the mishap as God's intended signature. While taking Job 17:5 to heart, and guarding against flattery through the years, I have found immense comfort and empowerment in the fruit that comes from His wounds and His bruises, which Job's writings and exchange with God so vividly described so many years ago.[4]

———

I experienced one more Jordan crossing in that season, and it was another completely unexpected experience but essential, nonetheless, to reaching the other side and entering territory ordained by God. Before anything was in concrete, having consulted with the director of the Home Missions Department of Elim Fellowship and having contacted my pastor to hear what he thought, I knew it was time to ask my father, "What do you think?"

Cell phones were not available yet, neither did students have phones in their rooms, but there was a phone booth in the foyer of the dorm that had a bi-fold door to close while making a call. After praying several days if not weeks about pastoring the church, I knew it was time to let my parents know what had been developing. They were quite understanding of the requirement to spend another year to complete the program, but it was time to communicate the sense of destiny the Lord was giving me to accept the invitation to pastor a small senior flock of His beloved sheep. I sat down on the little seat in the phone booth and closed the bifold door behind me. I still can hear the creek of the hinges as I pulled the door closed.

A tornado of memories and reflection whirled through my mind as I prepared to lift the phone and begin to dial. I had reflected often on the foolish days of my youth, a lengthy season that undeniably kept my parents worried, if not traumatized, which for many a father causes his love to be articulated through anger. I understood that, and only a few years earlier, both Jim and I were far from the pursuit of God. Now, running hard after God seemed a fad to Dad that he thought might burn out eventually. If nothing else in the meantime, it was to them a lot safer lifestyle they had grown accustomed to witnessing and dealing with. Now, it was about to involve a relocation with a thousand-mile separation and an unknown time frame. A few years prior, Dad might have appreciated that. But after having heard and experienced a repeated number of apologies and requests for forgiveness for our foolish behavior and disrespect, replaced by deference and esteem for them and their roles in our lives, Mom and Dad's hope of our return home was sincerely revived.

Sitting on the flat metal seat that was anchored to the wall in the booth, I picked up the phone and dialed home. I was prepared to accept my father's articulation of their hope that I would return home and find opportunity near them. I was not prepared for what I was about to hear. After laying it out and asking him what his thoughts were, the only words I can remember to this day are, "I think you need to swallow your pride and just come home!"

I have to say those words felt like a punch in the gut! I thought maybe I had not adequately described the particularly humble condition of the flock and its ailing facility, in one of, if not *the* most impoverished county in New York State.

At that time, I still was not sure my father understood the difference between what we were raised on in the Catholic Church and what a living relationship with God was about. But I was so convinced of his God consciousness and knew he could not deny the dramatic change and focus he was witnessing in his two sons' lives that I said, "Dad, I'm pretty sure you understand 'the will of God.'"

Looking back, I have to briefly reflect on my dad's personal history. My father's father battled with alcohol, eventually driving him to abandon his family in the early days of the Great Depression. Dad was only five years old then, and he accepted early the responsibility of being the male provider of the family. He sold newspapers on a cold, Chicago street corner on the South Side. Our grandmother, a hard-working single mom, managed to raise two successful sons, though she was wounded by the abandonment of a husband and father she and her boys would never see again. Those realities have their effect. One of the effects on our father was to motivate him to care and provide for his family in a way he had not experienced when he was a child. Thirty-five years of climbing the ladders of Sears Roebuck & Company would see all four of us kids born in different cities, until finally settling in New Orleans, *and eventually* moving to Atlanta. Now, it was Dad's hope that, if ministry was to be our calling and vocation, surely there would be plenty of opportunities in Atlanta or, at least, closer to home than Central New York.

When I credited him for understanding the will of God, it was evident that to him my words were religious jargon. I was hoping for his approval and some validation, but though I did not receive either then, I realized he was hopeful that I would come home where we might enjoy each other's company a little more than those earlier years had provided. After returning from those years of self-absorbed living and rebellion toward his values and hopes for Jim and me, our relationship with Dad became healthier than it had ever been. It was painful now to be wrestling with what I knew to be the "call of God," a call for surrender to His agenda and not mine.

Not long after Dad and I talked, I came across what Luke recorded of Jesus' teaching on discipleship.

If you want to be my disciple, you must, by comparison, hate everyone else—your father and mother, wife and children, brothers and sisters—yes, even your own life. Otherwise, you cannot be my disciple.

— Luke 14:26 NLT

On the surface, our English translation of those words of Jesus (originally in Koine Greek) seem harsh, but they are not. Jesus was prioritizing Kingdom of God followership and in no way diminishing one's love for and responsibility in family relationships. Truth is, when one has surrendered completely to Him in sonship, discipleship, and followership, the relationships with family can only accelerate and become more fulfilled according to our Father's intention and design.

I decided I would extend what was going to be a brief visit home before returning to New York. I stayed for nearly three to four weeks before returning. I have to believe that, when I headed back north, by then Dad had settled in his heart that I was doing the right thing, and I had his full support.

Upon return, I found a little, one-room cabin to rent along Seneca Lake, just north of the church. During that first summer, I got more involved with the small body of believers and found ways of making new connections, particularly with unbelievers in the community. When fall arrived and school reconvened, I drove up to Elim on Monday evenings to be at school all day each Tuesday and returned home after class Wednesday mornings. Then I returned on Thursdays for classes, spent the night, and attended classes Friday mornings before returning to the church after lunch every Friday.

After the first year with that initial elderly flock and several newcomers to the church, we agreed as a body to respectfully bury the old and bring in the new. With sincere respect for the years that the people had labored together and the many lives who were positively affected, there was also ample reason to "baptize" the work, close the door on the past, and step into a new day for the new things the Lord was about to do. We literally decided to "baptize" the church and replant with the newcomers and the old. We made a slight change to the church's name, which became identified as Bethel Fellowship Church.

I would serve for nearly four years as a single pastor until Nancy and I were married and spent our first year together, sharing the joys and challenges of a relaunched and growing church. As I would discover years later, planting a church from scratch, while very challenging in many ways, was free from the many deeply rooted conflicts that would continue to identify the church to many until those memories would be replaced by a new season of life and ministry in the community.

That first year together in marriage and ministry also found us preparing for the birth of our first child, Jenna, and it provided us with many opportunities to grow together in our relationship with God. As that year would draw to a close, we were feeling that it was time to take another step of growth in church planting and discipleship. We accepted an invitation from a seasoned church planter to work with him to develop a network of church plants in Central New York associated with their main campus in Syracuse.[5] We knew that this would not be a long-term commitment, but we labored together as though it were our assignment till Jesus returns. We did feel that we would return to the Finger Lakes Region or, more specifically, the Southern Tier in the not-too-distant future to plant a church in Corning, New York. We both sensed that there were some lessons to learn in the meantime, and after two years in Syracuse, we agreed to help two different Bible Colleges in Texas in the development and discipling of their students. One was IBC, the first Bible school I attended. While there, helping to complete an enormous 58,000-square-foot student center and serving as the dean of men, our second daughter, Jessica, was born!

Overall, those beginning years of ministry and marriage taught us both to lay aside all our assumptions of what ministry would involve, or what we might *want* to do or be, and to allow the Lord to take us by the belt and lead us where we might not choose to go, surrendering to what and where He had designed and planned all along.

Wanting to get this lesson across to His disciples, Jesus initiated a Q-and-A session one day with them, asking them this: "Who do men say that I, the Son of Man am?"[6] Their response was to offer several names that had been floating around. "Some say John the Baptist, some Elijah, and others Jeremiah or one of the prophets," they replied.[7]

Then Jesus asked the second question: *"But who do you say that I am?"*[8]

Peter was quick to the draw and answered: *"You are the Christ, the Son of the living God."*[9]

Jesus' response to Peter was amazing! He began by saying:

Blessed are you, Simon Bar-Jonah, for flesh and blood has not revealed *this* to you, but My Father who is in heaven. And I also say to you that you are Peter, and on this rock I will build My church, and the gates of Hades shall not prevail against it.

— Matthew 16:17–18

And as if that was not enough, He continued:

And I will give you the keys of the kingdom of heaven, and whatever you bind on earth will be bound in heaven, and whatever you loose on earth will be loosed in heaven.

— Matthew 16:19

Jesus was still not done! He continued by telling the disciples gathered around Him that they were not to tell anyone that He was the Christ. And then He proceeded to open to them what had been written in the prophets, but like most Jews of their day, they failed to see the suffering sacrifice that He would be when He came to fulfill the destiny He had embraced in eternity past.

Addressing this subject, Jesus

began to show His disciples that He must go to Jerusalem, and suffer many things from the elders and chief priests and scribes, and be killed, and be raised the third day.

— Matthew 16:21

When Peter heard Jesus describe what would take place in Jerusalem, his response was:

Then Peter took Him on one side and started to remonstrate with Him over this. "God bless you, Master! Nothing like this must happen to you!" Then Jesus turned around and said to Peter, "Out of my way, Satan! You stand right in my path, Peter, when you look at things from man's point of view and not from God's." Then Jesus said to his disciples: "If anyone wants to follow in my footsteps he must give up all right to himself, take up his cross and follow me. For the man who wants to save his life will lose it; but the man who loses his life for my sake will find it. For what good is it for a man to gain the whole world at the price of his own soul? What could a man offer to buy back his soul once he had lost it?"

— Matthew 16:22–26 Phillips

Jesus would speak similar words to Peter as Peter stood on the shore of the Sea of Galilee the day of that post-resurrection encounter with him and six other disciples who had returned to the familiarity of their trade in the face of their grief and confusion over what had happened to Jesus:

Very truly I tell you, when you were younger you dressed yourself and went where you wanted; but when you are old you will stretch out your hands, and someone else will dress you and lead you where you do not want to go.

— John 21:18 NIV

John went on to say in verse 19, "Jesus said this to indicate the kind of death by which Peter would glorify God. Then he said to him, 'Follow me!'" (NIV).

Undoubtedly, while John was clarifying that Jesus was referring to the *death* Peter would die, John was also underscoring what Jesus had spoken over Peter and his fellow disciples earlier in their journey together, and Jesus was reaffirming His promise to those who would give up all rights to themselves to take up their cross and follow Him.

We will address further in a later chapter Peter's receiving the release from the shame of his denial of being one of Jesus' disciples, but for now the lesson is the overarching fulfillment for those who will find the life Jesus promises when they *lose* their lives in exchange.

Ultimately, this is the *lostness* we are born to find! For the one who *"loses his life for My sake will find it!"* Emptiness and lostness would mark all humanity in the fall of man, when—in God's paradise of His presence and companionship—man chose to find his life on his own, and as promised, he lost it. Apart from God, man's lostness will continue to revisit throughout one's life, ever exposing the emptiness, uncertainty, and foreboding barrenness of one's soul, till alas it finds oneself through surrender to God.

Once the heart is regenerated by its surrender to God and His divine purposes, following Jesus as His disciple will require continual surrender to experience His everlasting freedom from the lostness of one's soul. How easily we can be enticed to pursue our own objectives and vision, achievements, accomplishments, even in ministry and while serving the gospel's missional objectives. But like a lamb being led to the Shepherd, as David so accurately defined, the Shepherd is the One who provides, leads, guides, gives rest, restores, deals with our enemies, pours out His joy upon us while extending His goodness and mercy, as we follow in His presence.[10]

---

1. John 14:18. In the King James Version, this verse reads, "I will not leave you comfortless: I will come to you." Other translations use words such as, "I will not leave you as orphans" (HCSB), or "I will not leave you orphaned" (MSG). Young's Literal Translation says, "I

will not leave you bereaved, I will come unto you." And the J.B. Phillips translation says, "I am not going to leave you alone in the world—I am coming to you." Like forgiveness, continuing to surrender to our orphan spirit, a trait of the Adamic nature, is a life-long practice. Holy Spirit continues to remind us when the chains of either bondage, both unforgiveness and/or the independent spirit of the orphan, come near. Leading and guiding us into truth, He nudges us when the temptation to renege our freedom or when the momentary pleasure of rebellion or resentment knocks on our door.

2. The usual "talk of the town" concerning the formation of the Finger Lakes Region with its characteristic north to south lakes that cover the northwest and central region of the state is they were the result of the alleged Ice Age, a theory derived from the ideas of evolution, in contrast to the Bible's record of the history of creation and God's decision to flood the earth in its early history and repopulate the earth, beginning with the sons and wives of Noah (see Genesis 6–9).

3. I had become friends with a dear Mennonite brother. He also had to complete his internship before graduation. He had returned to finish school from Guatemala, where he had served for two years after a catastrophic earthquake that had left devastating destruction a few years prior. He was already fairly fluent in Spanish, and knowing I had spent some time in Mexico and wanted to return, he asked me if I wanted to apply with him to serve our internship with the Mennonite Disaster Service, which was engaged in a similar disaster-relief service in Mexico. Though I was not Mennonite, he was confident that my experience as a carpenter and my having a reasonable grasp of Spanish might be a door opener for me. We prayed together about the possibility and applied. We were both accepted, and the day after Christmas of 1976, we boarded planes from our respective towns and then met in La Paz, Baja California, to serve in a disaster response ministry, with much gratitude to the Mennonite Central Committee and MDS (Mennonite Disaster Service) for resourcing the entire mission. The village we were assigned to assist was called Ocho-de-Octubre (the 8th of October), named after the day a hurricane had dropped ten inches of rain in a matter of hours over the mountains just south of La Paz, causing a flood so severe that it cut a path through the city of La Paz much like a razor would cut its was through a man's beard. We were building bathrooms by day, and by night we looked for opportunities to minister to those who had lost family members in the flood, as well as their homes, and were living in temporary cardboard huts.

4. Growing up, I stuttered, which was a big contributor to my insecurity and reluctance to even talk to friends, much less a teacher or other adults. My father repeatedly would say to me, "Slow down, son," though in my mind, there was a backlog of words that just could not find their way out. It was not until a few months after I had encountered the Lord that I realized I rarely stuttered anymore, and when I did, it was mostly over awkward words than every word! When I read the scripture that was accidentally changed from 5:17 to 17:5, I had to look up the word *flattery* to understand it. Essentially, it is the use of "excessive and insincere praise, given especially to further one's interests" (from Oxford Languages). I accepted the warning then and have witnessed its insincere practice just as its definition defines!

5. Saied Adour was a respected pastor and father in the Faith to many in the Elim community of churches and ministries. He was known particularly for his pioneer spirit and experience in church planting. He was an American born Lebanese, who when attending Elim as a student, met his wife, Esther, the founding president's granddaughter and the daughter of the then current president, Carlton Spencer. Pastor Adour's legacy speaks profoundly of his humility and passion for lost souls. He endeavored to see them come to know and grow in the Lord, and planted within a community of brothers and sisters in Christ, from which they themselves could affect a lost and hurting world.

6. Matthew 16:13

7. Matthew 16:14

8. Matthew 16:15

9. Matthew 16:16

10. Psalm 23, often memorized by children growing up in church, doesn't become real in our lives until we acknowledge we have gone astray and need to be found. Isaiah said, "All we like sheep have gone astray; we have turned, every one, to his own way; and the Lord has laid on Him the iniquity of us all" (53:6). Isaiah further goes on to define the cumulative transgression of all mankind, and its deserving penalty and punishment were taken on by Jesus. "Yet it pleased the Lord to bruise Him; He has put Him to grief. When You make His soul an offering for sin, He shall see His seed, He shall prolong His days, and the pleasure of the Lord shall prosper in His hand. He shall see the labor of His soul, and be satisfied" (Isaiah 53:10–11a).

Chapter 10

Threshold to Another Dimension

"Jeff, I think you should let this guy get around us. He's driving pretty crazy, and I think he's high on something," my wife, Nancy, said.

It was raining, and we were driving in rush-hour traffic on I-95 in Fort Lauderdale, Florida. Riding with us in our minivan was our youngest daughter, Laurel, then eleven years old. We were headed together to a college basketball tournament where our middle daughter, Jessica, was playing during her Christmas holiday. The traffic was moving unexpectedly well, pulling us along like trout in a stream during spawning season.

In our vehicle, we could feel the bass woofers from a young man's candy-apple red Honda Civic as he would get close behind us or maneuver around to Nancy's side of the car. I was driving in the farthest left lane on an eight-lane highway—four lanes headed north and four going south. My co-pilot for this journey (and many others) was engaged in suggesting that I might want to allow this young man to pass us.

"Where's he going to go?" I asked as he pulled alongside, again hoping to somehow get around me. "There's a tractor trailer right behind me, and I have no room to surrender!"

When he came alongside us, Nancy could look down and see the driver, a young man no older than in his early twenties, if that, and he appeared to be nodding his head, as if he were fighting to stay awake.

Suddenly, he dropped back behind us, between our van and the tractor trailer, and began to drift back even more, one car length, two car lengths—until he was several car lengths back. No one was filling in the space, which puzzled me for a moment, as I was glancing back every few seconds to see what was happening around me. Totally unexpectedly, with nearly six or seven car lengths between us, he careened into the six-foot concrete divider that separated us from the southbound lanes. His car turned completely perpendicular to the lane and began to roll, much like a scene in a movie intentionally created for effect. But this was no movie.

Car parts began to fly in every direction as his small Honda Civic, with more plastic and fiberglass body parts than metal, was being demolished. Within seconds, the tractor trailer that had been directly behind him—moving along at a minimum of the assigned speed limit, which was sixty-five miles per hour—was unable to avoid hitting him. It smashed directly into the young man's car. It appeared to me (for the fraction of seconds that I could glance in the mirror without jeopardizing our safety) that the tractor trailer was forced to drive completely over him. At what point the truck was able to come to a stop, I will likely never know, but it was clear that there was no way the young man was going to have survived that tragedy.

I instantly felt nauseous, causing me for just seconds to flash back to when I was only eight years old and had witnessed death for the very first time. I had seen a pedestrian, who had attempted unsuccessfully to cross a busy highway in New Orleans, lying in a pool of blood, with a sheet covering his body, except for his feet, which were sticking out from under the sheet. The traffic on that day in New Orleans had come to a near halt as we passed the tragic reality of someone who so unnecessarily met his death in his attempt to cross the highway on foot.

I had witnessed death many times since that day, but none returned me to the sickening, queasy feeling of unnecessary tragedy. While I was thinking thoughts and wondering why—why had the young man been driving so aggressively and why, if in fact he was under the influence of some stimulant, or alcohol, or whatever, had he chosen to take on rush-hour traffic on the highway dubbed "Death Valley"—it hit me. My daughter Laurel was sitting in the back seat of the van and had turned around, watching the entire time as the tragedy unfolded. She, like me at eight years of age, had just witnessed death. *What is she thinking? And how will she process this experience? What thoughts were racing through her mind as she watched in real time a tragedy of such proportion?*

I began asking the Lord what to tell her. *What can I say that will make sense of what she has just witnessed, watching it straight on rather than watching it through the rearview and side mirrors that Nancy and I did?*

And then the Lord spoke very clearly to my spirit, one of those occasions when there was no denying His "still small voice" deep within the spirit He has given us to know and communicate with Him. He said, "You can tell her that what she just saw, the closing moments of that young man's life, could be summarized in three things."

I felt for a moment that I was in a classroom. The God of All Creation was about to write on a blackboard three significant points that I would want to hold on to for a lifetime. I was tempted to pull over, but there was no way to maneuver that at the time. So, I listened as He spoke to me, "Tell her the young man's life consisted of three things."

I sat up so alert in my soul and spirit as these next words came forward, "Making choices . . . sowing seed . . . and choosing friends."

I was already in tears, grieving the needless and disastrous end of this young man's life. He was a son to his parents, a brother possibly to his siblings, a grandson to his grandparents, and a friend to his friends. More specifically, I was crying because of the pointless loss of his young life and crying because the three things the Lord had revealed to me made more sense than I could ever have imagined in that moment.

I didn't spend much time contemplating the word before sharing it with Laurel. I felt rushed in my spirit to help her process what I knew would not be easy, nor should it have been just shaken off as if she were only watching a movie. This was the real deal, a life had just stepped into eternity, and she had witnessed it happen.

Without delay, I delivered to her what I had just received from the Lord. I said, "Laurel, I just asked the Lord to help me share something with you that could help you process what you just saw."

She was very quiet as I retraced my steps with the Lord in that moment, as if we were walking with Him in the garden in the cool of the day, walking and talking with Him as He shared His wisdom with us both.

"He told me to tell you that this young man's life you just watched step into eternity could be summarized in three things." I paused for a moment to gather my emotions and then continued, "He said, 'His life could be summarized or reviewed by these three things: making choices, sowing seed, and choosing friends.'"

For an eleven-year-old, Laurel was already very insightful and had a genuine concern for others. It was apparent she was thinking and pondering what each of these things would mean to her and, more particularly, to the young man. We talked about his most recent choices that put him in the place he was in. More than likely, those choices were built upon many earlier choices—his choice of vehicles, for example, and his choice to use something that would affect his stability, state of mind, and destination that day.

I continued to review each of the three things God had spoken to me, and I continue to review them to this very day. I know this was not the first time Laurel had pondered the gift and responsibility of making choices, but this day shed light and understanding on that concept in a new way. I explained how free-will or the privilege to make choices is a God-given opportunity and responsibility as every choice has its corresponding effects and consequences.

Making choices. My mind raced through the number of choices that day alone that had led to this young man driving a Honda Civic, a car made popular among young people during the craze of the movies *Fast and Furious* and *Gone in 60 Seconds*. Popular they were, but a Civic was not the safest car to be driving aggressively on the highway known for more accidents on the East Coast than any other. Choices—wow! As deep as that concept was to me then, I couldn't stop on that image alone.

Sowing seed. I reflected for a moment how most of the seed we sow is unconsciously done, unlike the seed we intentionally sow in hopes of yielding the fruit of each seed. But we are sowing seed every day, all day long, and its fruit is sure to yield a crop, whether good, bad, or ugly. I cited the verse,

> Do not be deceived, God is not mocked; for whatever a man sows, that he will also reap. For he who sows to the flesh will of the flesh reap corruption, but he who sows to the Spirit will of the Spirit reap everlasting life.
>
> — Galatians 6:7–8

Choosing friends. I could not help but personalize this phrase as I had definitely been influenced by friends that I chose to allow to help shape my values, at least until the Lord arrested me and I surrendered to Him. I thought about how the young man might have been under the influence of something that altered his everyday level-headedness and drove him to drive as he had. *But then seeing him drift back as far as he had, before careening into the concrete divider, did he pass out? Was he on a legal medication? What really happened? I wondered. And had his choice of friends helped him create an envi-*

ronment *of influence that affected his choices, his premature destiny in life, and ultimately his death?*

From that day on, these three realities that are a constant part of our everyday lives continue to run through my mind and heart as I reflect on our discussion at hand. The gift of thought, the ability to think and process ideas and concepts, leads us to the choices that we make, the seed that we sow (consciously and unconsciously), and the very people we choose to associate with and, at some point, label as our friends.

Chapter 11

The Next Dimension—The Companion Disciple

FLASHING BACK TO MY EARLIER DAYS AS A believer—in fact, the very first time I stepped into a gathering of genuine believers at Life & Praise Tabernacle in Atlanta—I was quite intrigued by their reception, kindness, warmth, and sense of connectivity with one another. It wasn't hard to feel accepted and "right at home" among them.

The religious tradition that I had been raised in was not nearly as warm and relational. This alone was quite appealing and likable, and I found myself wanting to be in the company of this people as often as opportunity afforded. I wasted no time, therefore, settling into the routine of "meetings," attending both morning and evening services on Sunday, and whatever was planned during the week as well. It helped me to stay focused on my newly found relationship with God and gave me a family of believers whose lifestyle was a lot healthier than the practices of many of my associations of the past. With that environment pretty much behind me, and five hundred miles helping to separate me from my past relationships and patterns, I dove right into a new culture of what I knew was a much better choice for not only my survival, but my growth and development in God's purpose for my life.

After some time, I began to recognize an interesting trend, which probably should not have surprised me as much as it did. The truth is I was smiling so much every time I showed up at church or a church gathering that most of the youth of the church wondered what I was up to! I was truly overcome by the joy of the Lord, and it affected my whole disposition, something I couldn't explain at the time if I tried.

In addition to a whole new outlook on life and its purpose, I was very thankful to be in a robust culture among people whose interests, motives, and influence were generally healthier and more transparent than what I had been accustomed to. All I could do was smile with gratitude!

Soon, however, I began to recognize something interesting about the relationships I was witnessing, and it was this: The primary basis of everyone's connection and bond was not always the Lord but, oftentimes, something else. In other words, some seemed to have more of a bond of *common interests* than the bond realized by their relationship with God. There was nothing wrong with this, per se, but after a while, I began to see that these connections were not leading them into a more purposeful walk or connection with God, at least not as far as I could tell. Actually, I realized that the *snare of lostness* was lurking beneath the surface of many such connections, and time would soon disclose its grasp on different individuals.

Now, let me just pause here to clarify that it is important to understand the difference between "judging another" and "discerning" what God has planned and intended for you. Had I been "judging" what I was witnessing, I might have openly commented on it and made statements that this practice was wrong, or something to that effect. But discerning is something different, wherein we recognize when a particular (cultural and otherwise harmless) practice is not necessarily the most conducive for one's growth in the Lord, just as athletes are careful about their diet, their training routine, and their rest habits.

I came to understand early on that the church was the place for all kinds of people at all points of their walks and journeys with God, and it was certainly not mine or anyone else's business to "judge" them on their condition or their spiritual diets, training habits, rest patterns, choices of entertainment, hobbies, or the bases of their connections with one another in the church. But I could see that all of these *had both their positive and their not-so-positive components.* And this was something I continued to witness and even experience throughout my growth and development. I recall one experience in particular when serving with the Mennonite Disaster Service in La Paz, Baja California, Mexico, for a two-month internship.[1]

La Paz had been hit by a late-season hurricane that left over a thousand families without homes and an innumerable loss of life. While endeavoring to help this community recover, our team experienced an unforeseen and very unfortunate incident that indelibly affected us for life. After weeks of grueling labor building sanitation facilities over primitive temporary amenities for the hundreds of homes that were destroyed in the storm, we took a day to visit a beach at the very base of the Baja Peninsula, now well known as Cabo San Lucas. At the time, there were no resorts yet canvasing what was then the remote beach of Cabo which we discovered. We found our way to a specific area on the beach recommended by locals, a paradise type setting, with some four hundred yards of beautiful sand amazingly situated between two massive rocky cliffs, like divinely positioned bookends.

Excited to hit the water and body-surf the waves and play some soccer on the beach, all but one of the team jumped out of the van and raced into the crashing Pacific waves as they came to shore. After thirty or so minutes, we retreated to the sandy beach, deciding it to be safer to play soccer before any of us got towed out to sea. The currents and undertow were more severe than I had ever experienced, and we were getting more beat up by the waves than enjoying the surf. The south tip of the peninsula was known for creating accelerated currents, undertows, and riptides, and that day was no exception.

There were three young Mexican students who had come from a Bible school in the mainland to serve with our team during their semester break. Their companionship was admirable, and their love for God and people was exemplary and encouraging. One of the three young Mexican brothers, Marcos, did not swim, but he did want to walk along the shore and stay in no deeper than shin-deep water. We had just finished marking off boundary lines in the sand to play soccer when the director of the team asked, "*Donde esta Marcos?*" Has anyone seen Marcos? He was just here—did he go back to the van?"

Then one of his friends, Turibio, said, "He was just walking along the edge of the water, wading," when suddenly we looked out twenty to thirty yards beyond the incoming waves to see that Marcos had been pulled out into the water and was struggling to keep his head above the waves.

The director shouted to both Turibio and me, and said, "Turibio! Jeff! You guys can swim. Do you think you can get to him to help him?"

Ignoring what we had already experienced in the water and its aggressive waves and currents, we both ran toward where we last saw Marcos and began to swim in that direction, trying to stay above the waves to see if we could find him. While we swam toward where we thought he might be, the rest of the team found a trail in the dunes and followed it up the southern rocky cliff in hopes of being able to see Marcos and direct us to where he was.

As Turibio and I were keeping one another in sight, trying to stay within ten yards of each other, we began to find ourselves being pulled southward, rapidly beyond where we last saw Marcos. We tried to swim back toward the shore, but by then, we were being pushed by the strong current directly into the massive rocks and coral formations. Pulling myself up on one of the rocks in hope of seeing Marcos, I could see nothing but crashing waves racing each other toward shore, and no sign of our dear brother.

Suddenly, I realized I could not see Turibio either. He was out of my sight. I could only hope he had been pulled further south around the stacks and pillars of huge rocks and had found a way to get back to shore. But I was trapped, caught in a crab-infested cove of rocks, high tide coming in, and no way out but to get back into the treacherous water, or find a way to climb to the top of the cliff, barefoot.

As I looked up, I could hear members of the team yelling to me, saying they would find a rope and lower it to me. But I knew I had to find a way to escape the rising water, and swimming back out would not be an option. I couldn't wait for a rope. I knew I had to start climbing to get above the rapidly incoming tide.

I don't remember having as much fear for myself as much as a sense of defeat that we had not been able to find and bring our brother to safety. Somehow, I was able to reach the top of the cliff, fifty feet or more of lava-type rock with sharp edges and loose stones, some coming out in my hands or crumbling under my feet as I reached for a hold or stood on uncertain ledges, praying they would be secure and not break away and drop me to the rocks below. I will forever know I was not alone as I climbed that cliff but had been granted our Father's supernatural assistance, somehow enabling me to do what I was incapable of doing myself. As I reached the top, three of the team members pulled me up onto the ledge of the rocks.

"*Me ahogo*," they were saying, repeating what Marcos had said, "*Me ahogo!*" When they had reached the top of the hill, they could see him just for a moment struggling and crying out, "I am drowning! I am drowning." Like a sword thrust through my heart, I felt the loss of a precious brother, lamenting we had not been able to help as much as we tried and wanted to. Together, we would have to accept that God had chosen to take our brother that day, and we could have little to say but what Job himself had said in response to his great loss, "Naked I came from my mother's womb, and naked shall I return there. The Lord gave, and the Lord has taken away; blessed be the name of the Lord."[2]

I won't deny that I would wonder for some time to come why Marcos, of anyone, no more than seventeen or eighteen years old, drowned that day. Marcos was an undeniable evangel with a passion to share his joy of knowing Jesus and his freedom from lostness. Every night, the locals would find their way to the quaint patio of the humble quarters where we were staying to stare at the little black-and-white box television. Gazing at whatever program was playing, with eyes fixed on the tube, Marcos would engage the neighbors and capture their interest and concentration as he backed himself up to the television to lower the volume and share the gospel with them.

Why Marcos, Father? Why Marcos? The answer that would slowly emerge in my spirit was that he was undeniably ready to see the Lord, face to face. His amazing example would not easily or quickly fade, neither would his model and influence on not only his two *compañeros* he had brought with him, but on the others he had influenced back home, as well as our team and those we had witnessed receive his love and concern for them. We had only known him for the short time we served together, helping those without shelter, food, or sanitation. But my often reflected takeaway from the privilege of having walked with my beloved brother and sown the imperishable seed of our Father's amazing grace and love was to reach as many as possible within our grasp, ignoring the evident obstacles and challenges and uncertainties of life, wherever we may be.

Marcos certainly didn't know that this trip would cost him his life. The truth is he had already surrendered his life and was willing to go wherever and do whatever Jesus was going and doing, and to be who he had become in Christ to the world he was in. His influence was real, and like Abel of old, "he being dead still speaks."[3]

Marcos had entered into a dimension of *companion discipleship*. It's called the *power of influence*. His influence upon us all was a good influence, but sometimes the influence of others is not for good. The influence people can and do have on us often affects the choices we make, the seed we sow, and of course the friends we identify with. Conversely, whether we realize it or not, we are equally as "influential," affecting the choices those we influence make, as well as their sowing, reaping, and choice of friends. That said, let's look at two stories in the Bible that help us see the positive and negative of one's influence.

––––

Jesus had three friends who were siblings—Lazarus and his two sisters, Mary and Martha. It was Mary who had anointed Jesus with fragrant oil and wiped His feet with her hair. Lazarus had fallen ill, and his sisters sent word to ask Jesus to come. When Jesus was made aware of His friend's condition, discussion immediately arose between His disciples and Him over whether it was smart for Him to return into the region of Judea where He could be apprehended and even stoned. John's Gospel records the event:

> Now Jesus loved Martha and her sister and Lazarus. So, when He heard that he was sick, He stayed two more days in the place where He was. Then after this He said to the

disciples, "Let us go to Judea again." The disciples said to Him, "Rabbi, lately the Jews sought to stone You, and are You going there again?" Jesus answered, "Are there not twelve hours in the day? If anyone walks in the day, he does not stumble, because he sees the light of this world. But if one walks in the night, he stumbles, because the light is not in him." These things He said, and after that He said to them, "Our friend Lazarus sleeps, but I go that I may wake him up." Then His disciples said, "Lord, if he sleeps he will get well." However, Jesus spoke of his death, but they thought that He was speaking about taking rest in sleep. Then Jesus said to them plainly, "Lazarus is dead. And I am glad for your sakes that I was not there, that you may believe. Nevertheless let us go to him."

— John 11:5–14

At this point, Thomas made a statement that reveals one of the most remarkable traits of a *companion disciple*, if not *the* most, a trait that is truly notable and often found where there is a genuine relational bond between brothers and sisters in Christ. Before we consider this attribute of the companion disciple, let's remember the setting in which we find it disclosed.

It's very clear in this account from John's Gospel that, despite the disciples' knowledge of Jesus' great love for His friend Lazarus and Lazarus's two sisters, Mary and Martha, this idea of returning to Judea to see Lazarus was extremely disturbing to the disciples. They knew that Jesus would be putting Himself in harm's way, and likely themselves as well, and that He could very well be arrested and even sentenced to death. But amid their deliberation over whether He should go or not, Thomas, most often referred to by many as *the Doubter*, showed a side of himself that I've never heard commented on. John recorded it like this: "Then Thomas, who is called the Twin, said to *his fellow disciples*, 'Let us also go, *that we may die with Him.'"*[4]

That single verse is loaded with insight concerning the bond of courage that inspired Thomas, particularly while among his *fellow disciples*, to charge them with the challenge, "Let us also go, that we may die with Him." Some have suggested that Thomas was being sarcastic, as if to add further credence to their belief that, if Jesus had returned to Judea at that time, He would have been arrested and sentenced to death. But I don't believe for one minute this was what Thomas was doing. To the contrary, he was making a direct challenge to his *fellow disciples*, emboldened by their camaraderie and their shared companionship with Jesus.

I want to stress that we often draw strength from our companions in the Faith, even amazing strength, that might not otherwise exist, just as Thomas did on this occasion. How many times have we boarded the bus with at least one or more of our fellow disciples, bound for a destination we would likely never have signed up for were it not for the inspiration and encouragement infused in us by our brothers and sisters in the Lord? And how many times have you and I found strength to overcome a temptation because of the strength we drew from our fellow disciples standing with us at the time? Or how many readers can admit walking out of the woods of lostness, escorted by a companion whose confidence boosted theirs to follow the unseen trail to safety and back to the familiar ground of security?

Sometimes it's the imminent and far-reaching repercussions of a potential moral failure, and the impact that it could have on those with whom we have sojourned in the gospel, that help us stand erect, like the tree aided by the ropes till its roots are strong enough to withstand the gusting winds on its own.

That's the positive side of one's companion discipleship. But with every positive, there's an equally forceful negative dimension that we must be aware exists. John's account of Jesus' post-resurrection encounter with several of His bewildered disciples early one morning on the shore of the Sea of Galilee uncovers for us the potential negative side and the limitations of one's companions related to following the Master.

> After these things, Jesus showed Himself again to His disciples at the Sea of Tiberias, and in this way He showed Himself. Simon Peter, Thomas called the Twin, Nathaniel of Cana of Galilee, the sons of Zebedee, and two others of His disciples were together. Simon Peter said to them, "I am going fishing." They said to him, "We are going with you also." They went out and immediately got into the boat, and that night they caught nothing.
>
> — John 12:1–2

These truly loyal followers of Jesus—disciples of not a mere man of God, but the very Son of God, who "became flesh and dwelt among us," having beheld His glory, "the glory of the only begotten of the Father, full of grace and truth"[5]—now faced choices. Their choices would determine the outcome of the message they had received from the Lord of Glory Himself and the mission He had commissioned them with.

One can only imagine the overwhelming impact witnessing Jesus' arrest, torture, and crucifixion had on His disciples. Jesus had extensively prepared them for His prophetic destiny as Messiah, which had also been clearly detailed and foretold by Isaiah the prophet. However, when it so violently unfolded before them, with no means to stop the force of its brutality such that "His visage was marred more than any man,"[6] the disciples found themselves stripped of hope and thrust into a cavern of lostness they had never experienced. We can find chronologically recorded in the Gospels fourteen times that Jesus specifically described what would happen to Him regarding His suffering and crucifixion. This was a consistent theme Jesus sought to bring to their understanding of the Messiah's redemptive call and mission on His first Advent as the Son of Man, the Lamb of God, Emmanuel, God with us.

> From that time Jesus began to show to His disciples that He must go to Jerusalem, and suffer many things from the elders and chief priests and scribes, and be killed, and be raised the third day.
>
> — Matthew 16:21

Peter, as you may recall, revolted and told Jesus he would not allow these things to happen to the Master. You might have thought that Peter would have remembered the rather forceful rebuke he received from Jesus over his focus being more earthbound than heavenward. Jesus was apparently calling Peter to a higher understanding of what he could conceive or even imagine at the time. Rebuking and correcting him strongly, Jesus drove the lesson home by stating that Peter's focus and perceptions were of earthly and natural values, and not those of God's perspective and concern. Peter would need to draw from that lesson later when he would be faced with the decision of what to do when his Master would in fact be taken from them as Jesus had precisely defined.

Now, having been present during Jesus' arrest, His interrogation, His unimaginable scourging, the mockery and charade of a trial and sentencing, and having witnessed the indescribable anguish of his Master's crucifixion, not to omit his own denial of being Jesus' disciple while warming his hands by a fire, Peter found himself at a complete loss for what to do. Now, with six other (*companion*) disciples at his side, he made the statement, "I am going fishing."[7]

Lostness—that uninvited tormentor of the soul—it's the unforgiving terror that can suck the very breath out of our lungs and cause our hearts to race as if running to escape death's jaws. But now Peter's choices are not kept to himself, or his seed protected from the surrounding elements, while his friends watch him make the move that will become their lead to follow.

Much has been taught and heralded in the last number of years through many on leadership and its related concepts and principles. *The oft overriding principle of them all is simply this: the power and effect of influence on others.* But rarely, if ever, is heard the caution of one's negative influence. An influencer's ideas and example can impact another away from God or from God's directives. And in Peter's case, clearly, returning to his past and its familiarity in the face of indescribable discouragement and confusion seemed to him, and hence to six other companion disciples, to be the right thing to do.

Yet Jesus had not finished His discipleship training, nor was His mentoring and encouraging completed. Standing on the shore of the Sea of Galilee, just before the very sun which He had created made its debut at dawn, the resurrected Christ Jesus called out to seven of His twelve disciples who had followed one another back to the nets that would only catch mere fish and said, "Children, have you any food?"[8]

There are always more reasons than we can perceive this side of eternity why Jesus did the things that He did before returning to Father and sending Holy Spirit to continue His work within us and among us. This occasion at the shore carries so many insights and lessons, a few of which stand out to us in the context of our consideration, and surely many more that Holy Spirit can make known to us as He wills. One is that Jesus was returning to encounter His disciples to further reveal and confirm His Father's purpose in His crucifixion, death, and burial, and to pronounce emphatically the reality and significance of His resurrection, which was very much in question by His disciples. In addition to this, Jesus was giving Peter an opportunity to experience the forgiveness he must have craved since his plummeting into the well of denial, a well that Peter had so forcefully declared that he would never draw from.

And yet, we cannot overlook or underestimate the value of disciplines that come to Father's sons and daughters who have known the reality of regeneration by the Holy Spirit and who purpose to walk with Him intimately day by day. One of the certainties of being truly His is He will not only advocate for us against the enemy of our souls, the one who accuses us before our God day and night,[9] but He will lovingly confront the human tendency in us to go astray as sheep,[10] wandering into the pastures of lostness to pursue the predispositions and tendencies of our own souls rather than the gentle promptings of Holy Spirit. Peter and his companions were about to experience one such lesson of divine discipline, and Father chose to use a frustrating night on the sea of Galilee to launch the lesson. After several hours of unsuccessfully laboring at the trade these seven men could normally do blindfolded, they found themselves even more discouraged, fueling the lostness and sense of guilt and shame, having nothing to show for their toil.

> But when the morning had now come, Jesus stood on the shore; yet the disciples did not know that it was Jesus. Then Jesus said to them, "Children, have you any food?" They answered Him, "No." And He said to them, "Cast the net on the right side of the boat, and you will find some." So they cast, and now they were not able to draw it in because of the multitude of fish.
>
> — John 21:4–6

On this occasion, one must make room for divine intervention (or interference) in arranging for a frustrating night of fishing. In the same way that Jesus could instruct Peter to go down to the water and pull out the first fish he caught and there find a coin with which to pay their taxes,[11] He was now rerouting Peter and his companion disciples' intended catch for when He was good and ready to make it happen!

After toiling all night, with no fish to show for their labor, Jesus was about to turn their simple obedience to His instruction to cast their net on the right side of the boat into a prodigious and unforgettable catch of a lifetime. Not yet aware it was He who was standing on the shore, preparing a fire on which to cook their breakfast from what they were about to pull into the boat,

> The disciple Jesus loved said to Peter, "It is the Lord!" Now when Simon Peter heard that it was the Lord, he put on his outer garment (for he had removed it) and plunged into the sea.

> — John 21:7

What unfolds in the remainder of this story reveals that Jesus was absolving the very choices His disciples had made in the cruel shadow of His atoning sacrifice on their (and all humankind's) behalf. Peter would be the centerpiece of the goodness, mercy, and forgiveness Jesus would dispense, not only to him but to his *companion disciples* who had followed his wandering astray. Peter would become a model of one who learned from his confusable choices and whose unhelpful influence was turned around to reflect his restored faith, virtue, perseverance, and love in the face of rejection and even death.[12]

Indeed, this post-resurrection encounter holds for us examples of traits of both the *companion disciple* and the yet to be pondered *communion disciple,* the latter being the next dimension of discipleship. The remainder of John 21 reflects the further elements and characteristics of a deeper measure of our Father's desire for us to become His *communion disciples,* which we will discuss in the ensuing chapters.

---

1. See note 3 on page 94, regarding my mission here.
2. Job 1:21
3. Hebrews 11:4
4. John 11:16
5. John 1:14
6. See Isaiah 52:13–15 and Isaiah 53 in its entirety.
7. John 21:3
8. John 21:5
9. Revelation 12:10
10. See Isaiah 63:6 and Matthew 18:11–14.
11. Matthew 17:24–27
12. Peter's Epistles are encouraging directives, penned under the inspiration of Holy Spirit by a man who knew denial and failure, so very contrary to his intentions and desires, but was fully restored and forgiven. He reflects the intentions of our Father's design to regenerate the sons of God and bestow His very nature upon us with a living hope through the resurrection of Jesus Christ. A slow read of both Epistles by a hungry and open reader will bring to life specific instruction and guidance for a lifetime of following Jesus!

Chapter 12

Convinced of His Love

UP TO THIS POINT IN JOHN'S GOSPEL, THE disciple who was resting against Jesus' chest, during what has come to be known as the Last Supper, had been identified simply as *"the other disciple."*[1] Now, for the first time in John's record, this disciple is further identified as *"one of His disciples, whom Jesus loved."*

> Now there was leaning on Jesus' bosom one of his disciples, whom Jesus loved.
>
> — John 13:23 KJV

Whether a maturing believer in Jesus or one recently encountered and embraced by Him, it won't be long before you hear someone suggest that Jesus seemed to love this disciple (John, the writer of this Gospel) more than He did any of the other disciples. After innumerable readings of the New Testament and study of the Greek text, one will not find any substantive basis for such an idea, other than the manner in which John, accordingly dubbed *the Beloved*, wrote of the things he personally witnessed, heard, and experienced pertaining to Jesus and the Father He had come to reveal and represent.[2] A careful walk through the passages that might be construed to suggest that John was possibly more endeared to Jesus' heart than any of the others will more likely reveal after it is all weighed and measured that John simply had a clearer view and measure of understanding of *how much* Jesus loves us, and hence, him! The New Testament refers to that kind of experience as *revelation*, an unveiling of truth that requires the Spirit of God to unlock its treasure.

Simply put, *John got it!* He got it, and it deeply affected him. This is the most momentous revelation of them all—that our Father loves us with an unfathomable, immeasurable love and that love changes everything else that could possibly affect us this side of eternity!

John was experiencing a dimension of love that could only be conveyed and made real by God Himself, who, in the Person of Jesus Christ, had come to embrace all who would receive it and believe it.

There is minimal record, if any, of John's upbringing, family environment, childhood, or youth. We can assume that his mother might have been considered a little "doting" when she requested of Jesus that her two sons, James and John, be allowed to sit on Jesus' right hand and left hand in His Kingdom.[3] I would see her request as being that of a loving mother who wanted the most for her sons. But the love John was experiencing in Jesus was an overwhelming, overflowing, overtaking dimension of acceptance, belonging, and security that affirmed his relationship with the Son of God and his Heavenly Father.

John had been granted an understanding of Father's great love for us, made known to us in the Person of His Son Jesus, through whom John was experiencing an internal transformation of who he himself was while, at the same time, grasping more and more of the nature and character of God as they were being revealed through this Man for whom John had abandoned all to follow! Therefore, John took advantage of every opportunity he could to press in closer than others and stay longer with Jesus whenever he had the chance to do so!

I believe what John experienced awaits each of us who recognize, as did he, that there is something more for us— that fortune awaits the ardent miner of our Father's vast and limitless mercy, grace, and love! And that His undeserved grace and love will be lavishly bestowed upon us when we press past the crowds to just touch the hem of His garment.[4]

There's no doubt to me that in every believer's journey there comes a ground swell that discloses all the components of what can be called a *Christophany*, a personal and intimate event between you and Jesus that captures your understanding of His Person, His divine nature, and His purpose in our lives. His amazing love becomes a pivot for subsequent growing and increased intimacy with Him, as John so well described in his Epistles (letters) to the early church believers.

What marvelous love the Father has extended to us! Just look at it—we're called children of God! That's who we really are. But that's also why the world doesn't recognize us or take us seriously, because it has no idea who he is or what he's up to. But friends, that's exactly who we are: children of God. And that's only the beginning. Who knows how we'll end up! What we know is that when Christ is openly revealed, we'll see him—and in seeing him, become like him. All of us who look forward to his Coming stay ready, with the glistening purity of Jesus' life as a model for our own.

— 1 John 3:1–3 MSG

With that in mind, the transforming attributes of this dimension of discipleship are incredibly valuable to consider as we walk with the Lord. The disciples who recognize there is perpetually more and pursue such will reflect several recognizable characteristics as they commune with the Lord and abide in Him and His unending and unfailing design to conform them to the very image of His Son.[5]

---

1. Other [or another] disciple was used in John 18:15–16 and 20:4, 8. The disciple whom He [or Jesus] loved was used in John 19:26, 21:7, and 21:20. The other disciple whom Jesus loved was used in John 20:2.
2. See 1 John 1:1–4.
3. See Matthew 20:20–28.
4. See Matthew 9:18–26; Mark 5:22–43; Luke 8:41–56.
5. A verse often quoted, Romans 8:28, says, "And we know that all things work together for good to those who love God, to those who are the called according to His purpose." As encouraging as this is, we read on and discover why! Verse 29 says, "For whom He

foreknew, He also predestined to be conformed to the image of His Son, that He might be the firstborn among many brethren." It is clearly God's intent to transform us into the very image of His Son, and this process begins the very moment we are regenerated by His Holy Spirit and born spiritually of our Heavenly Father, as Jesus explained to Nicodemus in John 3.

Chapter 13

Hears His Voice

JOHN COMPREHENDED, EVEN IF ONLY IN A MINUTE measure, that Jesus loved *him*! He took possession of a most gratifying understanding that he was in fact loved by this Man, this God-Man, who was sent by our Father to "break-it-down," to make it real and understood by whosoever would receive Him.

Moving on from that factor of the *communion disciple*, we take the next step with John to discover what he was granted, as are we, the capacity *to hear the voice of the Lord*! The setting was the *Last Supper*, the name given to the last time before His crucifixion that Jesus would sit down with His disciples to break bread and model the spirit of a servant by washing their feet after the meal had been served. In John 13:14–15, we read His words to them:

> If I then your Lord and Teacher have washed your feet, you also ought to wash one another's feet. For I have given you an example, that you should do as I have done to you.

It wasn't long after Jesus had shared these words with His disciples that "He was troubled in spirit, and testified and said, 'Most assuredly, I say to you, one of you will betray Me.'" [1]

Those words lit an emotion bomb in the room, as His disciples began to squirm in their souls, *Who could such a disciple be?*

Now there was leaning on Jesus' bosom one of His disciples whom Jesus loved. Simon Peter therefore motioned to him to ask who it was of whom He spoke.

— John 13:23–24

Did you ever wonder why Peter asked John to ask Jesus whom He was referring to, rather than just asking Jesus himself? I don't think Peter was concerned about protecting the alleged traitor from embarrassment or exposure, nor do I think it was because John was seated closer than he was. I had wondered about that for a long time until, one day, the light went on! The issue here was simply this: Peter trusted John's ability to get a word from Jesus more than Peter did himself! In other words, *as a communing disciple, John notably had an ear for the voice of the Lord!* Peter did not ask Jesus directly himself because Peter trusted the relationship that John had with Jesus more than his own. Surely, he thought, *John should be the one to ask Jesus, "Who would be the one to betray Him?"*

It's amazing to me in our prophetic Christian cultures that some would prefer to receive a prophetic word defining and directing what their next steps are to be rather than developing an ear to hear the voice of the Lord as He intends. Jesus said, "My sheep *hear My voice,* and I know them, and they follow Me."[2]

The *relational culture* that Jesus obviously wanted to develop with His disciples was one in which every sheep and follower was able to hear His voice and follow Him. This is not something that is dependent upon a mass movement of people, all moving in an assumed direction like a school of fish, mimicking one another's cues in which direction to follow next! No, quite to the contrary. God's plan for us is that we be in *intimate communion* with Him personally, wherein He has enabled us to hear His voice, understand His will, and follow Him. *"My sheep hear My voice, and I know them, and they follow Me!"*

What's amazing to me, and I have to include this in this segment, is I just got a call as I was writing. The caller is a dear friend, a very humble man who helped us for years with innumerable automobile challenges. With five drivers in our home (my wife, our three daughters, and myself), it was not often that we were *not* repairing one vehicle or another!

Before this precious friend had moved to another state, we would speak frequently. But not having heard from one another for a quite some time, he gave me a call to share with me what he felt he had *heard* from the Lord. He went on to explain what he had received from the Lord, and I just had to laugh and rejoice with him over what he had shared with me. I explained to him that I was just writing about specific characteristics of a communion disciple, and specifically being granted the privilege and capacity to hear the voice of the Lord! And he called!

I received his call and what he shared with me as a nudging endorsement of my need to share this simple truth. I was laughing while we were talking, as I explained to him that my wife and one of our daughters had gone shopping on the first rainy day of our vacation, allowing me some time to get some writing done. I told him, "That's awesome! You can't believe how timely your call is! I'm actually writing right now about that specific characteristic of a communion disciple, that they *'hear the voice of the Lord'*! This is too much!"

He closed our conversation by telling me that I had better get my pencil moving so I could include that in what I was writing!

Peter's deferral to John to get the word from Jesus instead of asking Him directly himself was not the only record of John's hearing Jesus' voice, to which others would subsequently respond.

As reflected earlier, considering the manners of the companion disciple, Jesus chose to meet with a majority group of them who had resigned themselves to return to fishing, making it the third encounter with them before His ascension to His Father.

Early that morning, Jesus waited on the shore for the seven disciples who had toiled all night and caught nothing. He said to them, "Children, have you any food?"[3] We looked at this very passage earlier, alluding to the effect that one's example and influence can have upon us (and we on them) to sometimes move in a direction that may not have been in God's design and intent for us. Now, there's another lesson to behold, obscure, simple, but notable as we reflect on this dimension of discipleship.

In response to Jesus' question, they answered, "No." He in turn responded to them, saying,

"Cast the net on the right side of the boat, and you will find some." So they cast, and now they were not able to draw it in because of the multitude of fish.

— John 21:6

Now, in similar fashion as what had occurred at the supper table, "the disciple whom Jesus loved said to Peter, 'It is the Lord!'"[4] Note, there were six other companions on deck, but none other recognized the voice of the Lord.

It seems clear that the only follower of Jesus on board the boat that early morning who would recognize His voice, as He stood on the shore waiting to reveal Himself once again to those He would love to the end,[5] would be John, the disciple who identified himself as "the disciple whom Jesus loved."[6]

You might consider this a coincidence, or you can follow the trail of this disciple through the remaining record of his account to recognize the benefit of perception and duty that this follower portrayed.[7]

Having heard John announce, "It is the Lord," Peter wasted no time in diving into the water and swimming the hundred yards to the shore. His passion to see Jesus and his grief over his denial and its shackle of shame would meet with his risen Savior, Master, his loving Friend, who would forgive him and restore God's call and destiny for the remainder of his life on earth. While giving him the face-to-face opportunity to confess his devotion and love to Jesus not once, nor twice, but three times, in keeping with his three-time denial of Him, Jesus lifted from Peter the weight of his shame, as He revalidated his spiritual call and appointment for the apostolic mission he had been destined to fulfill, even unto death.

While so doing, Peter couldn't resist asking Jesus, "But, Lord, what about this man?" referring to "the disciple whom Jesus loved."[8] As Jesus responded to Peter, so also does He respond to us today, *"If I will that he remain till I come, what is that to you? You follow Me."*[9]

God's unique and distinct design and purpose for each one of us can only be realized in that personal and cherished encounter and walk with Jesus. Prophetic words of encouragement and exhortation may come and go, but in essence, as Paul defined the temporary nature and sometimes even failure of such, these cannot replace the glory of every child of God's respective intimate connection and delicate conversing with Jesus. *"My sheep hear My voice, and I know them, and they follow Me."*[10]

---

1. John 13:21
2. John 10:27–28 KJV
3. John 21:5
4. John 21:7
5. See John 13:1.
6. John 21:7
7. John (the Beloved) is credited for not only this Gospel, but also three Epistles, and the book of Revelation, which was given to him while he was exiled on the isle of Patmos after his captors could not burn him in oil.
8. John 21:20–21
9. John 21:22
10. John 10:27

Chapter 14

Courageous to Stand

THERE ARE TIMES IN OUR JOURNEY WITH JESUS
when we find ourselves seemingly standing alone against a
tide that feels as though it is going to take us with it. There
are no companions at our side or in reach to help anchor us
in the storm of temptation, affliction, loss, or whatever else.
The only anchor in these times that can steady the ship in
the storm that threatens to dash us on the rocks is the
confidence of Jesus' presence and the strength we draw from
the communion of His closeness and power.

In the intense heat of the threatening circumstances of
the hour, Peter found himself facing what could have been
the same furnace of brutality, torture, and even death, as
Jesus faced. Peter's concern and love for Jesus compelled
him to follow the posse that had come to arrest Him, but
unlike John, he chose to distance himself from being identified as one of Jesus' followers.

And Simon Peter followed Jesus, and so did *another disciple.*
Now *that disciple was known to the high priest,* and went with
Jesus into the courtyard of the high priest. But Peter stood
at the door outside. Then *the other disciple,* who was known
to the high priest, went out and spoke to her who kept the
door, and brought Peter in. Then the servant girl who kept
the door said to Peter, "You are not also one of this Man's
disciples, are you?"

— John 18:15–17

By now, we understand that the "other disciple" and "the
disciple whom Jesus loved" were one and the same man, the
writer of this Gospel, John himself. Before we can imagine
why John chose to remain as unidentified by name as he did,
we must remember that "no prophecy of scripture is of any
private interpretation [origin], for prophecy [Scripture]
never came by the will of man, but holy men of God spoke
as they were moved by the Holy Spirit."[1] That said, as John
was writing the account of what he and his fellow disciples
experienced with Jesus, he was guided by Holy Spirit to pen
his identity to the reader as he did. He had obtained such an
identity from his understanding of God's overwhelming love
for him, now being demonstrated by this Man on trial
merely for claiming to be the Son of God.

Now, having followed the detachment of Roman soldiers
who had come to arrest Jesus and bring Him into the very
courtyard of the high priest, where John was already known
as a follower of Jesus, John saw Peter standing outside the
gate and proceeded to see if he could get him in. Peter,

knowing well that their goal was nothing less than crucifixion for Jesus, kept his distance as he watched from outside the courtyard.

John approached the servant girl, the one responsible for the door into the courtyard, to request that she allow Peter access. As Peter entered, she spoke the words that would set the stage for what Jesus had already said would occur. Riddled with fear, unlike any he had ever experienced, not only for Jesus, but for himself, words that he would likely never forget sounded in his ears: "You are not also one of this Man's disciples, are you?"[2]

Temptation comes in so many different forms. This form, seemingly so unfair, creates a current that can drag one's anchor behind the boat as it breaks away from the intended course of the soul. Before Peter could even think about the outcome of his words, or the measure of their impact, he found himself replying, *"I am not."*[3] This would be only the first of three denials that Jesus had told Peter he would pledge.

> I tell you, Peter, the rooster shall not crow this day before you will deny three times that you know Me.
>
> — Luke 22:34

John, the *"disciple, known to the high priest,"* had already accepted that, whatever judgment Jesus would receive, he would receive as well. Though that would not occur, John would cling to the very end to his soon-to-be-sentenced-to-death Savior, Friend, Son of God, Jesus.[4]

There is no record in any of the four Gospels whether John was ever questioned if he was *"one of this man's disciples."* The record is evident that John *was known* to be a follower of Jesus. Even before Jesus had embraced the cross on which He would offer Himself as the only acceptable atoning sacrifice to God for our sin, John had spiritually taken up his cross as a disciple of Jesus. With that, John had accepted its identity, along with any potential religious, cultural, or familial incrimination or consequences it would mean for him so labeled.

After denying being a follower of Jesus to the servant girl who kept the door, Peter found his way to the fire where the servants and officers who had arrested Jesus were warming themselves. While standing among them, they said to him, "You are not also one of His disciples, are you?" And Peter again denied it, and said, "I am not!"[5]

Finally, "one of the servants of the high priest, a relative of him whose ear Peter cut off, said, 'Did I not see you in the garden with Him?' Peter then denied again; and immediately a rooster crowed."[6]

I will forever remember the first time I introduced Nancy as my wife to someone neither of us knew. Now that we were married, she was no longer *merely* my girlfriend, nor even *only* my fiancé, but now she was (and is) my wife! Together, we understood that we had entered a covenant with God that He designed to be for life. I felt in that moment something that even the wedding day itself did not hold. I was *professing now*, both to those who knew us before and those we were yet to encounter, that I was no longer the man that I was, but I was now joined by God in covenant with my wife.

A wedding ring alone or a cross around one's neck carries no weight compared to the recognizable change in one's person and character that identifies them as being in covenant with God. Being a disciple of Christ, an identified follower of Jesus, does not conform to cultural trends incongruous with biblical truth or socially acceptable lifestyles that are contrary to Father's creation and design.[7] Many churches today are often fusions of professing followers who treat their walk with God much like their walk through the mall or perusing the internet, stopping to purchase what is trending, but passing on biblical values of life much more beneficial and favored by the Father with whom they attest to identify.

There may be a lot of people (believers and unbelievers) who know that you are a believer and that you identify yourself as a follower of Jesus, someone who claims to be in relationship with Him. But we should humbly remind one another that there will be times when to be identified with Jesus will cost us at the very least some social discomfort, possibly some scorn, even mockery, no doubt rejection, and perhaps at the most persecution or death.[8]

John was surely better prepared than his fellow disciples, fully surrendered to what potential consequences being an identified follower of Jesus would mean. Today, here in our Western culture, truly surrendered believers are surrounded by the accelerated denial and dismissal of a Sovereign Creator and Lord, whose attributes and absolutes have been exchanged for the god of one's own imagination and passions. John's courageous love is what we need as believing families are being assaulted by the idea of pervious truth, which leads to the rejection and denial of God's sovereign design for mankind's families and societies. The floodgates of compromise have been opened by socially mandated terminology intended to govern the morphing of the true nature and design of Father's intention in His creation into something altogether manipulated by foolish and darkened souls.[9]

Every day will present us with opportunities to mirror the reality of a loving and just Father, misunderstood and misrepresented by the grip of lostness. Our Father yearns to liberate the willing and surrendered from the chasm and pitfalls of sin and its global effects for which He gave His Son to redeem and set us free. Such dimension of discipleship, that purposes to center your life and its course in communion with your very Creator, not merely as a religious practice, but a fully surrendered bonding to Him as Lord and Father, will bring a continuous awareness of His love and sustained joy in your life. Your fully surrendered life of communion with the Father will also reflect itself into the darkness of your world and the world's cultural lostness to shine its light and direction to the many deniably confused, but visibly lost and suffering inhabitants.

---

1. 2 Peter 1:20–21
2. John 18:17
3. John 18:17
4. In 1887, hymn writers Anthony Showalter and Elisha Hoffman together wrote the lyrics to the hymn "Leaning on the Everlasting Arms." One verse to note: "What have I to dread, what have I to fear, leaning on the everlasting arms; I have blessed peace with my Lord so near, leaning on the everlasting arms."
5. John 18:25
6. John 18:26

7. "And do not be conformed to this world, but be transformed by the renewing of your mind, that you may prove what is that good, and acceptable and perfect will of God" (Romans 12:2).

8. "Yes, and all who desire to live godly in Christ Jesus will suffer persecution" (2 Timothy 3:12).

9. Read the first chapter of Paul's letter to the Romans. Then continue reading the entire letter, often!

Chapter 15

Cares for What He Cares For

HANGING ON A ROMAN CROSS DESIGNED FOR A brutally painful and torturously slow death, Jesus was about to surrender His last breath in full recompense for mankind's redemption for all who would believe and receive. But there was one more cherished concern He needed to address. Though Jesus had four brothers, He chose to entrust the care of his mother to John.[1]

> Now there stood by the cross of Jesus His mother, and His mother's sister, Mary the wife of Clopas, and Mary Magdalene. When Jesus therefore saw His mother, and the disciple whom He loved standing by, He said to His mother, "Woman, behold your son!" Then He said to the disciple, "Behold your mother!" and from that hour that disciple took her to his own home.
>
> — John 19:25–27

Nothing more affirming could be said to express the sacred trust and confidence Jesus had in John than to share these words among His last. And truly, there can be no greater responsibility and trust to bestow on a follower of Jesus than to be given, in some measure, the care of our Father's flock and family. More often referred to as one's call, the trust God bestows upon those whose hearts possess the Spirit of the Great Shepherd to care for His flock overrides the carnal tendencies of some who allow their calling to thrust them into avenues for recognition and personal approval. John didn't allow his calling to be driven by such carnal tendencies, and neither should you, should you agree to be overwhelmed and satisfied with a joy that enlarges and strengthens you for the role God chose to bestow upon you.

There's something to be said of the commission Jesus placed upon His mother as He extended her mother's heart to include this disciple who treasured Jesus and His love for all. An unknown measure of comfort was being administered by Holy Spirit to both Mary and John as the last phrases of the chapter of Jesus' life were being penned.

There's no biblical record of the days spent together, sharing the sorrow of their earthly loss of a son and a brother unlike any other. John no doubt accepted the high call of caring for the mother of Jesus until the day that she would be received into the glory of His presence in heaven. John, however, would be taken and tortured and attempted to be boiled in oil at the hands of Rome's tyranny and rejection of the gospel message John lived to deliver. Instead, supernaturally delivered from the flames of persecution and torture, he was exiled on the island of Patmos, believed to be in his late 80s, if not early 90s. There he received an *enduring revelation* of the testimony of Jesus Christ, of "things which must shortly take place,"[2] and of His Person from eternity past, through the course of time, and into eternity future.[3]

Having already penned the Gospel of John and the three Epistles, he revealed that he and the disciples witnessed the manifested Word of God, God's dwelling among them, and His glory, "the glory as of the only begotten of the Father, full of grace and truth."[4] And though John had witnessed the transfiguration of Jesus with his brother James and Peter, he would now experience a dimension of *communion* with Jesus, intimately revealing Himself, that words alone would be incapable of revealing, like Ezekiel's description of what he had experienced: "This was the appearance of the likeness of the glory of the Lord."[5]

John would be kept from joining his fellow disciples, all of whom would die a martyr's death, except Judas, who like Esau, sold his birthright in exchange for something of no eternal value whatsoever.[6]

John's remaining days would model the very words he recorded that came from the mouth of the One he followed till the very end.

Most assuredly, I say to you, unless a grain of wheat falls into the ground and dies, it remains alone; but if it dies, it produces much grain. He who loves his life will lose it, and he who hates his life in this world will keep it for eternal life. If anyone serves Me, let him follow Me; and where I am, there My servant will be also. If anyone serves Me, him My Father will honor.

— John 12:24–26

John truly was honored by the Father, even before stepping permanently into His eternal presence. The very words of Jesus that John had recorded in his Gospel would be graciously granted John, and the island of Patmos would provide an Eden environment for *communion* between him and the One he chose to follow. Banished to the isle of Patmos by Roman authorities after their attempts to torture him to death failed, John would find a solace of *sustained communion with Jesus* as he would be charged to "write the things which you have seen, and the things which are, and the things which will take place after this."[7]

Sustained communion with Jesus, it's more than the goal or destination of discipleship. It's the great "treasure hidden in a field" or "the pearl of great price" that will cost us all.[8] In my own sojourn, I have experienced many moments of it in the hills and valleys, in the "Red Sea crossings" and the "valley of the shadow" wanderings, whereby all such experiences were designed and orchestrated by the One I have chosen to follow.

Only weeks prior to the release of this book, I was reminded again of the Master's call to follow Him in sustained communion. I was driving in my truck when I received a call from a dear fellow pastor with whom I had served for many years. Knowing I was about to lose cell signal for my phone, I pulled into a rest stop so we could finish our conversation. I told him that I was pulling into what I called the "rattlesnake rest stop." I had been calling it that ever since I learned that there had been rattlesnakes found in the garbage cans and on the property of the rest stop years before, creating a dangerous problem for travelers. The highway department eventually took some careful precautions to alleviate the danger of encounters with the snakes and to protect the public.

While there, I got out of my truck and walked over to the caution signs hanging on the carefully designed wire fences to keep the snakes at bay. I wanted to take a picture and send it to my friend, so I snapped a few quick shots.

When I was done, I walked back to where the truck was parked and finished my conversation on the phone. I put the key into the ignition to start the truck. *Click, click, click!* The truck's engine didn't turn over. I assumed right away it was likely a problem with the starter, so I crawled under the truck to do a test, lying on my backside. You might know there are tricks to bypass the solenoid and crank the starter without it. I tried, but I had no such luck! It was a beautiful Saturday afternoon, and I had a dozen other things yet to do, especially on the threshold of Sunday with its usual commitments and responsibilities. The last thing I needed was to be stranded in the rattlesnake rest stop!

As I lay under the truck, a severe temptation of frustration and its partner anxiety were pounding on the door of my soul! Not only was this a huge interruption to my schedule, but more importantly, I knew it would not be a smart place to be lying on my backside underneath my truck, even if I had the starter and the tools I would need to get it back on the road. I called my daughter Jessica who was working not far away and explained my dilemma. If I had the truck towed to a shop for repair, it wouldn't happen until Monday, as most shops are closed on the weekend. I asked her if she would come, pick me up, let me bring her back to her job, and allow me to borrow her truck. She agreed.

While waiting for her to come, I called another pastor friend of a church we had planted in the area years before. I asked him if I could have the truck towed there so I could install a new starter. He was gracious to welcome me to park it beneath a little grove of birch trees, and before long, I was lying underneath my truck, talking to the Lord.

Indeed, it was a beautiful late Fall Saturday. Saturdays for a pastor, or anyone serving in any ministry capacity on Sundays, hold the last hours of opportunity to gather what the Lord would have them serve the flock they might be attending to. It was becoming clear to me that whatever I had intended to do that day was being reassigned by the One who created me and had arranged my day as He is most entitled to do! On this occasion, somewhat like John the Beloved, I was about to experience, while on my backside underneath my truck, a Patmos isolation with God.

Communion began as God first reminded me of the setting He had created for Adam and how He had placed him in an unimaginable garden, the nature of which had not been touched by sin or decay. He also reminded me it wasn't His creation that He intended to captivate Adam and Adam's soon to be companion with, but it was His very own *Image*. I thought of the matchless pleasure of such *communion, knowing Him,* and walking together in the cool of the day.[9]

I will spare you the details of my work on the truck except to say the starter on this particular truck was squeezed into a very difficult, seemingly inaccessible location. It would have been hard to manage for any skilled mechanic who had a garage shop with a lift and all the tools required at his fingertips. Let's just say I was at a major disadvantage and totally unaware of what I had in store. I determined that I should listen only to the waves of God's presence and the breeze of the island He had prepared for our day together!

I have to confess I did not complete the job that day, though I would discover that much of what needed to be done would be best achieved with my eyes closed as access to the bolts that needed to be removed were completely out of sight! I waited to revisit our island of serenity on Monday, expecting more tranquility and peace and *communion with my Father* than what could easily have been a persistent cyclone of exasperation and vexation. The choice is in the soul, determining which nature we're going to allow to rule not only our destiny, but every waking step of the sojourn we have been created for.

In the process, I learned a lot. Not only about my vehicle, and conquering the job, but it was *another* reminder of how "being still, and seeing the salvation of the Lord, which He will accomplish for you today,"[10] has a transforming effect on one's demeanor, disposition, peace, and ability to overcome even the most challenging and oft considered impossible hurdles placed before us. But even more important, I understood anew of how eager our Father is to hang out with us, to commune with us, and to take walks through any trail available to Him and me, and you and Him. And He will go to great lengths to draw us to Himself so that we can enjoy Him and He us.

145

I chose this personal *day-in-the-life* encounter with God as we wind down this reflection of one man's discipling journey of response to Jesus' personal invitation to follow Him, because this encounter reflects an average day of one's life as well as the opportunity we have to accept each day as meaningfully designed connection with our Heavenly Father. Not many, if any of us, will have a similar walk with Jesus as did John the Beloved, or Peter for that matter, or any of the earliest followers of Jesus. But each of us can share the same escape from the darkness of lostness in our lives by accepting the liberating brightness of Jesus' life. John so well defined that life when he wrote: "In Him was life; and the life was the light of men."[11]

We can embrace Jesus' invitation to follow Him, regardless of the culture we have been placed in. And we can do this with assurance because He knows the way to God and the truth about God, and He is the very life that God gives. In Him, we have the blanketing coverage of all that we need —all that He has prepared for us—this side of entering our Father's house.[12]

In closing, there is no more truly astonishing, fulfilling, and gratifying existence known to the world than to surrender your life to the One who created you and follow the very Author and Finisher[13] of the only eternal life that can recover and restore you for this life and the life to come.[14] Your sojourn of discipleship will take you through the developmental days of *carnal discipleship* as you develop teeth for meat and become exercised in the elementary principles of the gospel.[15] Along the way you will find fellow or *companion disciples* who will be a must for your continued development and growth. But to fail to recognize that

Father's design shaped each of us with an emptiness that can only be satisfied by His intended pursuit of the only One who can love us like none other can lead one back into seasons of lostness and vanity, until surrender to His glory and majesty is once again restored to one's soul. Remember you were made for communion with Him—for sustained communion.

Many years ago, when a good friend and brother in the Lord and I were bidding each other farewell, having no idea when we would cross paths again, we charged one another with a departure note that has stayed with me (and he as well) to this very day. *"Keep it in Jesus"* was our charge to each other, and its reverb remains in our spirits. I leave the same with you now. Truly this is a journey, a sojourn Father has designed and planned, and one that surpasses any other pursuit or purpose for existing. May yours be one of a never-ending response to Father's drawing and ensuing guidance into His heart, mind, and purposes, both for this life and the life to come!

---

1. Mark 6:3 and Matthew 13:55 both identify the four brothers of Jesus: James, Joses, Simon, and Jude.
2. Revelation 1:1
3. In biblical terms, "Jesus Christ the same, yesterday, today and forever," expresses the truth of His eternal existence and deity, and His unchanging nature, authority, absolutes and attributes.
4. John 1:14
5. Ezekiel 1:28b
6. Genesis 25:29–34
7. Revelation 1:19
8. Matthew 13:45–46
9. Genesis 2:8 and 3:8
10. Exodus 14:15

11. John 1:4
12. See 1 Corinthians 2:9.
13. See Hebrews 12:2.
14. See 1 Timothy 4:8.
15. See 1 Corinthians 3:1–3.

About the Author

Jeff is a pastor and teacher whose life and ministry are marked by integrity, discipleship, and a genuine love for people. He and his wife, Nancy, have pioneered and planted several churches in the Southern Tier of New York and have served on staff in three Bible schools: International Bible College, San Antonio, Texas; Fountain Gate Bible College, Plano, Texas; and Elim Bible Institute, Lima, NY. He is a President Emeritus of Elim Bible Institute. Jeff and Nancy founded Mutual Faith Ministries & Network in 2013. Jeff tirelessly coaches leaders, pastors, and ministers, establishing them in their callings and missions.

 twitter.com/Jefaniah
instagram.com/jeffclark70x7

Made in the USA
Monee, IL
28 July 2023

40019630R00090